Lively Assemblies for Happy Schools

Margaret and Dennis Goldthorpe

Acknowledgements

Writing the acknowledgements is always a delightful task. There are, as usual, so many people to thank.

We should like to thank the staff and children of Alexandra School, who are always so willing to have a go at anything during Dennis's often rather lively assemblies (and you were all good at hockey, really!).

We should like to thank Corin Redsell, our patient and kind editor, especially for his forbearance over Margaret's incapacity to master emailing.

Lastly, we would like to thank our family – especially our children Katie, Sophie, Lotte and Tom, who have, as ever, been patient and uncomplaining with us as we, yet again, buried ourselves in the computers.

Lively Assemblies for Happy Schools
LL07087
ISBN 1 85503 380 1
© Margaret and Dennis Goldthorpe
Cover illustrations © Rebecca Barnes
Inside illustrations © Garry Davies
All rights reserved
First published 2004
Reprinted 2004

Printed in the UK for LDA
Duke Street, Wisbech, Cambs, PE13 2AE UK

Contents

Introduction
The ant, the helicopter and the careful gardener

Picture, if you will, an ant. No, many ants, all working away at building and maintaining their ant-hill. Tirelessly they are doing all the complicated and energetic things ants do, and they are doing them very well.

Unfortunately what they cannot know is that they are building their ant-hill in a pile of topsoil which is on the back of a dumper truck currently heading for a new flower-bed.

There's nothing wrong with what the ants are doing; it's just that they are too close to see the whole picture.

Now imagine the same scene from a helicopter. The helicopter is full of ecologists. They are concerned with biodiversity and they want to see a working ant-hill. The helicopter pilot swoops around the countryside. The ecologists have their cameras at the ready. All of them are clever, skilled and efficient at their jobs. Their understanding of the value of ants is faultless. They all have a truly spectacular view of the surrounding countryside and landscape.

Unfortunately what they cannot see is that a marvellous ant-hill is just below them, on the back of the lorry they have flown over several times, and that it is about to be destroyed by being tipped onto a flower-bed.

There's nothing wrong with what the pilot or the ecologists are doing; it's just that they are too far away to see the fine detail.

Sometimes as a teacher or headteacher we find we are in the dumper truck, expertly dealing with the details – the incident in the playground, the fancy new computer, the trying parent, the child who won't sit still in assembly, whatever. We can be so tied up with details that we don't see the big picture, maybe that the children are growing up rather parochial and unconcerned with the plight of those less fortunate than themselves, or perhaps with a limited understanding of their own spiritual life.

There again, we might find we are in the helicopter, worrying about league tables, national insurance costs, recruitment, OFSTED and action plans – losing touch with the details. Are the children quick to forgive? Do they share easily?

What we need is a way of going between the two. We need to be able to look objectively at the whole pattern of our lives, to make sure we are going in the right direction and also to find out how to manage the details that will make it a good life.

Perhaps we need a different perspective; perhaps we need to be more like a good gardener.

Then, we will alternately stand away to look at the whole, to plan how we want it to look; and then get in close, planting the garden carefully, paying great attention to the intricate balance between the vision of the completed garden and the welfare of all the plants and animals that live there.

We need to see the big picture. We need to look at our life as a whole and think about what we want it to look like. If we are passionate about justice, we need to be able to see how the world works and where and why injustice exists. Then we need to get in close, to be able to see how we can effect change, begin to make the things that really matter to us happen.

We don't want to be the ant with a life ruined through lack of vision; we don't want to be in the helicopter unable to get close enough to see what to do to make the vision a reality. We need to be the gardener. We need to have both the vision and the ability to make it happen.

This is the function of these assemblies. They are here to help adults and children alike to look at the world and think, 'What do we want the world to be like?' And they are here to help us to manage the detail that will mean that this life, this chosen and created life, becomes a reality.

Note that each assembly, except one, includes an optional Bible passage and prayer. A 'Thought for the day' has also been provided as an alternative way to end each assembly.

That's a weight off my shoulders!

Theme

The importance of forgiveness.

Preparation

Minimal. You will need the following equipment:

◆ Two ordinary children's school rucksacks. Two carrier bags are fine if no rucksacks are available.

◆ Six rocks! These can be bits of newspaper screwed up into balls, real stones, flints or even rocks from a rock garden. Paper will require some acting skills, real rocks won't!

The assembly

You will need two teachers to act in this assembly. That's probably you and a conscripted colleague.

Before the assembly, scatter the 'rocks' all over the stage or acting area. If they are bits of screwed-up paper you will have to explain to the children that they are supposed to be rocks.

The action for this assembly involves you walking along with your friend, your rucksacks on your shoulders. At first the rucksacks are empty, and you are walking along amongst the rocks, cheerfully chatting. You can either be yourselves or imagine you are children.

As you walk along, you start to argue with each other.

Each time one of you says something horrible to the other, the offended person puts a rock in their rucksack.

The idea is that the sadness you feel when someone is nasty to you is like a great weight that drags you down and makes life hard.

Dialogue

A: I got a good mark for my story.
B: Only because you copied me!
A: I didn't! That's horrible of you.

A picks up a rock and puts it in their rucksack.

B: Do you like my new shoes?
A: They're OK, I suppose.
B: Why only OK? What's the matter with them?
A: Nothing. It's just that they are a bit old-fashioned, really.

B then puts a rock in their rucksack.

Use appropriate arguments for the children in your school. If they are all currently arguing about trading cards or small craze toys, use those as examples. Make the arguments recognisable to the children as arguments they might have.

As you put more and more rocks in your rucksacks, act as if walking gets harder and more exhausting. If you have real rocks this will be easy!

Eventually, when all the rocks are in the rucksacks, stop.

A: I can't go on any more. I feel so tired, fed up and miserable.
B: So do I. What's the problem, do you think?
A: I think it's all these rocks.

Sit down and take out a rock from your rucksack and look at it together.

A: *(As if reading the rock)* This says 'Arguing about marks.'
B: That was me. I was really horrible to you. I shouldn't have said it. I am sorry.
A: *(Cheerfully)* That's OK. Let's forget about it.

Smile and put the rock back on the ground.

Continue taking turns to take the rocks out of your rucksacks, 'read' them, apologise and forgive each other, and get rid of the rocks that are in the rucksacks until both rucksacks are empty.

Both pick up the now-empty rucksacks and swing them onto your shoulders.

A: This feels so much better. Next time I say something silly, I will try to remember to say sorry straight away so I don't make you carry that great weight of misery around with you.
B: So will I!

A: And we'll forgive each other quickly as well!

Set off together again cheerfully.

The drama is followed by a question-and-answer session. During this no name is to be mentioned.

Come forward and talk to the children about what the little play means. Ask them what they thought the rocks were meant to represent. Ask them if they have ever felt burdened or have burdened someone else with a great weight of misery by being horrid and not saying sorry.

Get them to tell you how they have felt when someone has been nasty to them.

Explain that sometimes saying sorry can make a great deal of difference.

Ask the children for examples of times when they have felt sorry and have said so.

Ask them what would have happened if the upset person had not accepted the apology and forgiven them. If they need prompting, say that they might have gone on lugging the rocks around.

Explain that when we forgive, we help ourselves as well as the other person.

Explain that it is also very important to accept apologies with grace and to forgive the person who has upset you.

You might also like to say that if we pause for a moment to think before we speak so we don't say the awful thing in the first place, we will not have to go through any of this trouble.

Suggest that over the next week they try hard to think before they speak. If they do upset someone, they must try to be quick to ask that person's pardon . . . and then make sure they do not make the same mistake again.

Permission to Photocopy

Bible verses

Colossians 3, v12–14 (NIV).

Therefore, as God's chosen people, holy and dearly loved, clothe yourselves with compassion, kindness, humility, gentleness and patience. Bear with each other and forgive whatever grievances you may have against one another. Forgive as the Lord forgave you. And over all these virtues put on love, which binds them all together in perfect unity.

Prayer

Jesus said we would be forgiven only the same amount as we forgive others. Let's remember that as we say The Lord's Prayer:

Our father in heaven,
May your name be honoured,
May your kingdom come,
May your will be done on earth as it is in heaven.
Give us today the food we need.
Forgive us the wrongs we have done,
Just as we forgive the wrongs that others have done to us.
And do not cause us to be tempted,
But save us from the Evil One. Amen

Thought for the day

We all make mistakes. Each of us sometimes says unwise things or gets cross. Let us remember that we must stop and apologise if we have been horrible to someone. Let us also remember that we must accept other people's apologies and forgive them with grace.

Choosing time

Theme

Learning to make a conscious decision to be your best self even in trying circumstances.

This is a complex assembly that is best suited to Key Stage 2.

Preparation

You will need the following:
◆ Five top-year children.
◆ Five masks, comprising simple picture faces.
◆ Five photocopies of the script for the assembly.

There is no need to make complicated masks with eyeholes and so on. Just cut five ovals as large as you can make from A4, from fairly stiff card. The children can hold them up in front of their faces. If you have enough time and suitable materials you can put them onto sticks.

One side of each of the masks must have a smiley face. The other sides are different:
◆ two sad faces;
◆ one worried face;
◆ one scared face;
◆ one cross face.

This assembly can be as easy or as complicated as you want to make it. Its message, however, is not simple.

If you are short of time, line the children up and read the whole script to them. If you have time for a rehearsal you could divide the script up to give them each lines to read.

If you want, you can change the names and scenarios to fit your situation – for example a male teacher may not be quite so annoyed about being unable to use a hairdryer as a female would. Treat the scenarios provided as guidance.

You could replace the children with members of staff acting as children, which would make the scene much funnier – especially as you will get cross with them!

The assembly

Line up five children (or staff) with the smiley face side of their masks showing.

I have had a horrible morning! When I woke up I found there was a power cut, my alarm clock had stopped and so I had overslept. I couldn't wash my hair because the water was cold and I had no electricity for the hairdryer. All of that put me in a really bad mood.

On the road here, I realised I was running out of petrol. I had to go out of my way to get petrol and that made me even later.

Then, at the traffic lights, a stupid man hooted at me because he thought I was too slow getting away from the lights! How rude! He made me furious.

When I walked into school I was in a foul mood.

The first person I met was A.

Name one of the children with a sad face on the back of their mask. Go up to the child and speak by them.

They were smiling, and they said, 'Good morning . . . *[your name].*' All I could see was that they had tomato sauce on their jumper, so I shouted at them: 'Look at you! You look a right mess! Go and wash that mark off.' They stopped smiling and went off to dab at their jumper, looking sad.

The first child turns their mask round so that now the sad face is showing.

The next person I met was B.

Name the second child with a sad face on the back of their mask. Go up to the second child and speak by them.

They were peering in the fish tank and tapping their hand against the glass. They turned to me and smiled. I shouted at them, 'Leave that tank alone, you'll frighten the fish to death.' They stopped smiling and went off to find their friend. They were now looking sad.

The second child turns their mask round so now the sad face is showing.

After this I bumped into C.

Name the child with the worried face on the back of their mask. Go up to that child and speak by them.

They were by the library and smiled at me. I said, 'That whole library is a mess.

I want you to tidy it up at break. I'll inspect it at lunchtime.' They stopped smiling and went off to class looking worried.

The third child turns their mask round so now the worried face is showing.

Next I met D.

Name the child with the scared face on the back of their mask. Go up to the fourth child and speak by them.

'I have a job for you,' I said fiercely. 'Be outside my office in five minutes. Go and tell your teacher you won't be in registration, and be quick!' They stopped smiling and went off to their class looking scared.

The fourth child turns their mask round so now the scared face is showing.

Then I saw E.

Name the child with the cross face on the back of their mask. Go up to the fifth child and speak by them.

They were leaning against the wall in the corridor, right by a noticeboard. 'Have you been fiddling with that noticeboard?' I asked angrily. 'Look at it, it's all raggedy. You really are a complete pest.' They tried to say it was not them, but I didn't listen. I just shouted some more and told them not to tell fibs, even though I know they never tell fibs. They stopped smiling and went off to their class looking really cross.

The fifth child turns their mask round so now the cross face is showing.

I stomped off into my office – furious with the world.

A little while later, when I came out of my room to go to assembly, I saw all of these children again. They were all smiling!

The children turn their masks round again to the smiley sides. They don't need to speak; you can continue to narrate for them. If you are using staff, they can speak, poking their heads round the masks.

'What have you lot got to smile about?' I said, irritably.

Permission to Photocopy

'Well,' said A, 'I thought it was silly being upset with you. I decided you had a point; I did look rather messy. So I just gave my jumper a bit of a scrub and look, it's better now, isn't it!'

'I thought the same, it was silly being upset,' said B. 'I mean, I know you like the fish as much as I do and I didn't want to frighten them. In future I'll just look, and not bang on the glass. There was no need to be upset.'

'As for me,' said C, 'I looked in the library and I thought, She's right, it's a tip. I'll get a couple of friends to help sort it out. We can get it done at break. It'll look great when it's finished. Nothing to worry about.'

'And I thought,' said D, 'Well, she's never yet asked me to do a horrible job, so there's no need to worry.'

'As for me,' said E, 'I thought, Wow! She's in a right mood! She's not usually like that. And she knows I always own up if I've done something wrong. I never tell fibs. I felt really angry. But then I thought, I'll stay out of her way till she calms down, then I'll ask her if I can talk to her. I'll explain it wasn't me. Better to sort it out rather than get into a state. After all, she's not **usually** a horrible person.'

I felt terrible.

A few bad things had happened to me in the morning and I'd been really silly and taken it out on everyone.

I hadn't thought about being my best self.

But when I was horrible to these children they had been so sensible.

They didn't go off and take it out on everybody else.

I didn't think – I just reacted.

They thought – and they **chose** to be their best selves, even though it was difficult.

No matter what happens to us – however upsetting, or worrying, or scary or unfair – we can always **choose** to be our best selves and do the right thing. We should never let someone else make us be our worst self. We are in charge of our own behaviour at all times.

So remember: 'Choosing time' isn't something that happens just occasionally at school. 'Choosing time' is every minute of every day of our lives. We can always **choose** to be our best selves.

Bible verses

1 John 4, v7, 12, 16 (CEV).

My dear friends, we must love each other. Love comes from God, and when we love each other, it shows that we have been given new life. No one has ever seen God. But if we love each other, God lives in us, and his love is truly in our hearts.
God is love.

Prayer

Dear Lord, when other people are being unkind or difficult towards us, help us to think about how you would want us to behave towards them. Please guide us and give us the strength to do the right thing. Amen

Thoughts for the day

Everything can be taken from a man but one thing – the last of the human freedoms – to choose one's attitude in any given circumstance. *Victor Frankl*

There is nothing either good or bad but thinking makes it so. *Shakespeare*

You cannot choose how people behave towards you – but you can always choose how you behave back!

Count your blessings

Theme

Learning to open our eyes to all the things, big and small, that are a blessing to us.

Preparation

This assembly does require some preparation, and so it is not really suitable for a last-minute panic assembly. Shame – but there it is.

- You need to ask all of the staff if any of them collect anything: thimbles, pottery frogs, hedgehogs, plates, pigs, figurines, stamps, old books – anything; you just need a good, big collection. It would be ideal to have three or four different collections. Ask them to bring them in on the day before the assembly, so you are sure you have them.
- Ask the children if they collect anything – you will probably have better luck here. Again ask them to bring them in on the day before the assembly. Try to get two or three different collections.
- A flipchart and pens.
- A couple of tables for the collections.

The assembly

Ask the staff and the children to stand by the tables with their collections.

Have a chat with them about their collections. Find out how many items they have. You could ask them how long they have been collecting pink pigs, or whatever, and which item in their collection they like best.

You could ask them which piece they are most pleased with, which was the most difficult to acquire, if there are any stories attached to any of their collection and so on. You will probably have most luck with the adults on the interviewing front.

You are aiming to show the children that collecting things is fun and that people enjoy making new finds, acquiring something rare, and getting an unexpected bargain.

This next bit is important. Ask them again how many pieces they each have.

Get everyone to give them a big clap and ask them to sit down.

Now talk to the school. Explain that collecting things is fun and that it doesn't have to be expensive; it could be collecting shells on a beach.

Now tell them that you are going to start a very special collection in school.

This is going to be a 'Blessings Collection'.

Talk about what a blessing is. Use some examples of your own and take examples from the staff and children.

Make sure you differentiate between blessings and pleasures. Most blessings are pleasure but not all pleasures are blessings. Blessings are essentially gifts from God, so they are good for us. Many pleasures – like junk food, TV, Playstation games – are not blessings. Healthy food, good eyesight and working hands are.

Count your blessings

Explain that sometimes we forget to notice what a large collection of blessings we have and we forget to count them. But this week we are going to start collecting in earnest.

Tell the children that you are going to have a special noticeboard in the entrance hall/assembly hall, somewhere that is central and accessible to all, and they are to bring their blessings to the board.

Using the flipchart and pens, get them started on this. Ask them for some examples of blessings they have. It is very important to say that you want the children's own blessings.

We are not all blessed in the same way; for example some will not be blessed with grandparents or siblings, but they will be blessed with good health. Not all will be blessed with perfect health, but they might be blessed with an enjoyment of music or dancing.

Go for small blessings, simple things like listening to a story while curled up in a warm bed.

Ask the children to fill the noticeboard with examples of blessings like these:

- ◆ **Nature**: Pictures cut out of magazines of food, sunrise, sunsets, the countryside, pets, flowers, sunshine, rain, earth, animals, insects.
- ◆ **Our bodies**: Pictures of swimming, climbing, gym, sport.
- ◆ **Arts**: Singing, dancing, painting, colour.
- ◆ **Our homes**.
- ◆ **Our families**.

I am sure you can think of a million more; the list really is endless. Ask the children to get their families involved.

Tell them the Blessings Collection will be the biggest collection of all.

Bible verses

From Psalm 100 (NIV).
Shout for joy to the Lord, all the earth.
Give thanks to him and praise his name.
For the Lord is good and his love endures forever.

Prayer

Dear Lord, help us to notice all of the people and things you bless us with. Help us to remember to thank you every time we recognise a blessing – even if that's a hundred times a day – and let us be a blessing to others. Amen

Thought for the day

If I lived to be a million years old I wouldn't have enough time to count all of my blessings.

Different but the same

Theme

Remembering that it's differences that make the world exciting and it's love that makes it all worthwhile.

Preparation

You will need a selection of things that are 'different but the same'. We used the following:

◆ A collection of six nice ties.
◆ A selection of books.
◆ Six or seven CDs.
◆ Several school photographs.
◆ A box full of objects that you, or another member of your family, holds dear: children's books, old baby clothes, family photographs, old soft toys and so on.
◆ A selection of six children who have all agreed in advance to come onto the stage to be talked about. Make them as different from each other as they can be, in age, appearance, talents and personality types.
◆ A table for the collections.

The assembly

Hang the ties up on the back of a chair or display board.

Display the books and any other collection you have on a table.

Now you need to have a very brief chat about each of the collections.

You might, for example, explain that you wore a particular tie at a wedding and that another is a college tie, that one is an unusual tie bought for you by your mum, or your spouse, and that another is a tie you wear to school at Christmas time.

Then explain that they are all different, and they are all special, but in one way they are all the same – they are all ties.

Go on to look at the CDs. Again, briefly point out their differences and explain why they are all special, but point out that they are all CDs.

After looking at each of the collections, move on to the 'much loved' collection.

Explain that these are all toys (or whatever), but they are each very special to their owner. Take each one out and draw attention to it – maybe you could tell a story about each one. Go on to say that all the toys are special and all are unique, but they are all toys.

This is the tie I embarrass my family with.

Now call the selected children out from the audience and ask them to stand in line.

Go along the line, saying something positive about each child. Don't be critical, even in jest. Saying, 'And this is Craig, a right little monkey who has given me these grey hairs. Oh, but I suppose he's lovely really!' will not cut much ice with poor Craig and is not in the spirit of this assembly at all.

Instead, say something like 'This is Craig who draws brilliant cartoons.', omitting to mention that they are usually executed all over his maths book.

When you get to the end, repeat that, like the much loved toys, they are all different, all special. Send the volunteers back to their seats.

Explain that the point of today's assembly is that we have to remember that we are all different from each other. That is what makes us all special. Indeed, in our school we celebrate people's differences, looking for the thing that makes each one of us uniquely us.

Go on to say that you would never want to hear of anyone being teased, judged or gossiped about because they were different in any way from others.

Say that in this school, in one crucial way, we are all the same as each other. Ask the children in what way that might be.

They will probably say we are all children or people.

You can say that is true, but so is something else. **What makes us all the same in this school is that we are all loved.**

If yours is a church school you can explain that this is one of the most amazing things about God. He made us all different from each other, but he loves us all the same.

Bible verse

John 14, v2 (NLT).

There are many rooms in my Father's home and I am going to prepare a place for you.

Prayer

Dear Lord, help us to see that everyone has their own specialness.
Help us to be the kind of school where our differences are celebrated.
And, Lord, help us to know that you love our differences. You made each of us unique. But you love us all just the same. Amen

Thought for the day

Let us remember that if all the flowers were daffodils, if all the birds sang a thrush's song and if all the fish were cod, we would live in a dull, dull world. It's difference that makes the world exciting and it's love that makes it all worthwhile.

Song

Below are the words of a song that can be used in this assembly. The music for this song appears on page 16.

When God made me,
He had in mind,
The very same me
That you now find
Standing here, looking at you,
The very same you that he made too.
For we are all different,
As different as a splash in the deep blue sea,
Yes, we are all different,
But he wonderfully loves,
Yes, it's wonderful he loves,
Oh, he wonderfully loves
Both you and me!

When God made me

Words and music: Margaret Goldthorpe
Arranged by Anne Dudley

When God made me, he had in mind, the ver - y same me that you now find

Stand-ing here, look-ing at you, the ver - y same you that he made too. For

we are all diff - er - ent, as differ - ent as a splash in the deep blue sea, yes

we are all diff - er - ent, but he won - der - ful - ly loves, yes it's

won - der - ful he loves, oh he won - der - ful - ly loves both you and me!

Permission to Photocopy

Eat chocolate and save the world!

Theme

Learning about fair trade and its importance to poor countries.

Preparation

You will need to do a little bit of shopping and about an hour of baking. As this assembly could be the beginning of a long-term project for the school, it will need to kick off well.

Make about twenty-five fairy cakes. If they are anything like mine, it might help if you stick a blob of icing on the top of each cake. They need to be appealing. Put them on two baking trays.

Have available a bunch of ordinary bananas.

A basket of Fairtrade items bought from your local supermarket. Bananas, mangoes, pineapples, tea, instant coffee, ground coffee, cocoa, drinking chocolate, chocolate bars, fruit juice, honey, sugar and muesli bars are all foods that can be bought through fair trading schemes. The key Fairtrade item to buy is chocolate.

Some supermarkets stock more of these foods than others. If you have difficulty finding foods bearing the Fairtrade mark, try your local Oxfam shop; they should have a good range of Fairtrade tea, coffee, drinking chocolate and chocolate bars. You could try asking your local supermarket to stock goods you find unavailable.

The assembly

This assembly is about eating chocolate! It encourages you to eat chocolate – but only a special variety of chocolate.

First we have a little play.

Sit in an armchair, with a side table beside you, if possible with a lamp on it. The idea is that you look as if you are at home.

My name is Mrs Eliza Smith *(or any other invented name; you want the children to know that it is not you)*. I've had an awful week. On Monday morning I lost my purse and on Monday evening my car broke down.

Well, I can't fix the car because I've no money, and I can't get to work and earn money to fix it because I've lost my purse and I've no money for the bus fare.

I'm in a bit of a pickle here.

But I've had a really good idea. I'm going to make two trays of buns from ingredients in my cupboard.

Then I'm going to hand them to my neighbour Mrs Jones. She has a car and she is going to take them to your school.

You can buy my buns, I'll have the bus fare to get to work, and then I can save up and get my car mended!

Good, eh!

Get up and get the two trays of cakes.

Do you like them? They look good, don't they? I bet you can't wait to buy them!

Oh, here's Mrs Jones.

Another well-briefed teacher appears.

Hello, Mrs Jones, have you come to collect my cakes and take them to sell at school?

Mrs Jones: Yes. But I am going to buy them all from you. Then I am going to sell them at the school.

Wonderful. If you give me £1.50 then you can sell them for 10p each and we'll both make 50p profit.

Mrs Jones: Sorry, I'm only going to give you £1.05.

£1.05! You can't do that. That's not fair. They cost £1 to make.

Mrs Jones: Sorry. It's £1.05 or nothing. Take it or leave it.

But that means I'll only make 5p profit on the whole batch of cakes. I'll be weeks saving up for my bus fare at that rate. But, I suppose I'll have to take it. *(Look downcast but accept the money.)*

Mrs Jones takes the trays of cakes to the side of the stage. Another member of staff comes on.

Mrs Jones: Hello, are you Mrs Green, the school cook?

Mrs Green: Yes. Are those cakes for sale? How much are they?

Mrs Jones: £2.50.

Mrs Green: Thank you very much. That's 10p each. That seems very reasonable. The children will enjoy these. Can I have some more tomorrow?

Mrs Jones: Certainly. See you tomorrow.

Well, Mrs Jones came back the next day and the next. Sometimes she gave me £1.05, sometimes only 90p, sometimes £1.10. I had no choice but to take whatever I was offered. I worked as hard as I could – baking, baking, baking. But it took me two weeks to make 50p. I was never going to be able to fix my car or even afford my bus fare to go back to my job.

I was trapped.

Mrs Jones, however, had soon made £10. And she hadn't baked a single cake.

Do you think that was fair? Was that fair trade?

No. I don't think so either.

Now, I'm not really Mrs Smith and you know these ladies are not Mrs Jones and Mrs Green. And I do have a job and I'm not trapped. But this problem happens all over the world every day.

Get out your supply of bananas.

Take these bananas. Now, these bananas may well have a sorry history.

The person who grew them may have been forced to sell them at a tiny profit, or worse, for less than they cost to grow.

This kind of thing means that millions of poor farmers all over the world do not have enough money to feed their families, send their children to school or have clean drinking water. It means even their children are forced to work long hours with bad food and no pay.

Just like me in that play, they are often trapped. They have to sell their bananas, but the money they are given is very variable and often not enough for them to live on properly.

And, instead of Mrs Jones, there is often a big company taking all of the profits.

Now what can be done about this problem?

Permission to Photocopy

Well, we could send money to the poor farmers. But they don't want that. They just want a fair price for their bananas – as I wanted a fair price for my cakes.

But there is good news. There is an organisation called Fairtrade. This is its symbol. *(Hold up the Fairtrade symbol shown at the end of this assembly).*

If you buy anything with this mark on it, then you can be sure that the farmer has been paid a proper price. They will even have been guaranteed a small profit.

These three excerpts are from real letters written by people who sell goods through Fairtrade.

The teacher who played Mrs Jones can read this; it will re-establish her as one of the good guys!

'I work for farmers who grow bananas in the Dominican Republic. They sell them through the Fairtrade market. I've worked with bananas for twenty-five years. Things are good right now. We earn more money, and if we have problems we can solve them.'

'We have bought one truck and need another now. Every day we are working hard to do things better.'

'We really appreciate what the Fairtrade farmers have done. We hope that Fairtrade shoppers continue helping.'

Would you like to help those people? Do you know one way you can help?

Great news! The answer is – eat chocolate!

But only Fairtrade chocolate. Because to help the farmers we have to buy their produce and eat it.

Who would like to try some chocolate? *(Get a couple of volunteers to eat some Fairtrade chocolate.)*

Lots of food is fairly traded. Who would like to come up and have a dig in my shopping basket? *Invite a couple more volunteers to the front to have a rummage. (Talk to the munchers.)* Do you like chocolate? Do you like eating chocolate? Do you want a bit more? Now, this is tasty stuff!

As they are munching show the other items to the school.

Look at this sign again. I am going to give you one for each class. I want you to look out for products with this sign on them when you go to the shops. If you see any Fairtrade food, try to buy that rather than another brand.

Some products, not all, might cost 10p or even 20p more. You will have to decide for yourself if it's worth saving up a bit longer to buy something in order to help the farmers.

If you do buy anything with this sign, bring the empty packaging in to school and we will put it in a display.

Remember this? *(Show them the trays of cakes.)* Was what happened to them fair?

It wasn't, was it? Let's make sure when we buy things that we try to buy them from people who trade fairly.

Bible verses

James 2, v15–17 (NIV).
Suppose a brother or sister is without clothes and daily food. If one of you says to him, 'Go, I wish you well; keep warm and well fed,' but does nothing about his physical needs, what good is it? . . . faith, if it is not accompanied by action, is dead.

Micah 6, v8 (NIV).
And what does the Lord require of you? To act justly and to love mercy and to walk humbly with your God.

Prayer

Dear Lord, help us to remember that poor people in far-away places are just people like us who want to do the best for their families. Help us to find ways to help them do that. Amen

Thought for the day

Actions speak louder than words (or fine words butter no parsnips!).

Source: www.fairtrade.org.uk

Permission to Photocopy

I want it and I want it NOW!

Theme

The purpose of learning to work with diligence and tireless patience.

Preparation

You need to find at least six children with skills or talents that are good enough to show to the school. The key is finding skills that you don't have. If you share any of these talents, don't use them.

For example, you might find the following:
- A good skateboarder. That means one who can at least be sure of doing a reliable Ollie, to order. (Don't worry – they know what that means.)
- A good dancer, one who can do some move you definitely can't do. If you have a ballet dancer and a tap dancer you can use both of them.
- A footballer who can, for example, flick the ball up on his foot and do a few tricks.
- Anyone who can play a decent tune on an instrument. 'Twinkle, twinkle, little star' is fine. If you can find players for three or four different instruments, you can use any or all of them.
- A child who can draw or paint really well.
- A good cartoonist.
- Someone who can speak a second language.

Ask the staff to suggest suitable children a week before the assembly. If this fails, ask for volunteers a week in advance. I would hold a brief audition. Many children are ludicrously overconfident about their skills, which is lovely, but not much use when they have to come up with the goods in an assembly!

Ask the six children to bring to the assembly anything they may need for their demonstration: special shoes; a skateboard; a musical instrument and music; paper, pencil and paints; a ball – whatever.

The assembly

*The aim of this assembly is to demonstrate that it takes patience to succeed at difficult things. I am afraid you have to act as a bit of a klutz. The more enthusiastic yet hopeless you are, the better. But, **please**, don't even attempt anything that may cause injury.*

I wrote this assembly with the teacher as the useless article because I am not keen on those assemblies where adults stand up and tell children 'You won't get anywhere with anything in life unless you work hard.' Children know this. As that fulmination rarely comes with any real incentive, it rarely makes children want to work hard. It usually makes them either irritable or sleepy.

Even worse are the harangues where the adult tells the children a story about how the adult got where they are today by diligence. The implication is that if you work tremendously hard, you too can be an old person standing on a stage boring a load of kids to tears. The only time this works is if the adult does a job that children covet, but even with diligence 99.999 per cent of children are not going to grow up to play for Man U or be a pop star.

This assembly aims to preach the familiar message, the message that skill and success require hard work and patience, but it offers the celebration of existing successes as a spur. You are admiring the virtues of patience, diligence and commitment in order to encourage more of the same.

As I don't know which skills you will find in your school, I am going to give two examples. I think that will be enough for you to put the message over. You really need to play this for laughs.

I have often thought that I would like to be able to play in a concert or dance on a stage. Have you ever wanted to do that? I'd just like people to look at me and admire me. Wouldn't that be great? If people all went 'Aaahhh' with admiration at our skills?

Well, I've decided to make that dream come true. I've invited some of my friends here this morning and they are going to teach me how to . . . *(name the skills you have found).*

The first one is ballet dancing. I have always wanted to dance in the local dance festival. Rebecca *(or whoever)* is going to show us how she does ballet dancing. She is going to perform an arabesque for us. Then I will have learned how to do it and I can be in the festival! I can't wait!

The child runs across the stage and does an arabesque.

Oh, that's so good! That's just what I want to do! OK, show me again.

They do one more demonstration.

OK, I think I've got it. Oh, I can't wait to dance on stage!

You attempt an arabesque. If necessary, ham it up. Wait for the laugh.

How about that? Was I good enough for the local dance festival. No? Oh, how disappointing.

Never mind, I'll try something else. I know, I'll learn to play the violin.

Here is Jack *(or whoever)*. He can play the violin. OK, Jack, show me how it's done.

They do their 'Twinkle, twinkle, little star' or whatever.

Oh, yes! I want to do that.

Take the violin and attempt to play. This should raise a laugh.

Oh dear, I don't think I can really play in public. What a dreadful shame!

Again, show great disappointment at your lack of skill and maybe have another go. Then, as before, give up and go on to the next skill.

Do this with each of the skills.

Oh dear, all my dreams are ruined. I so wanted to be able to do some of these things. Perhaps I'll ask each of these children how they manage to be so good.

Interview each of the six children. Ask them how they manage to be so good at each activity. You might like to lead the discussion towards:
- *how many lessons they have had;*
- *how much time they spend practising;*
- *difficulties they have encountered and how they overcame them;*
- *the importance of patience and diligence.*

Do you think if I choose . . . *(pick something you might be able to manage)* and work as hard as these children, and have as much patience, I might be able to improve? I am going to try.

Does anyone have anything they would like to work at and then show us? *(Take a few suggestions.)*

You might like to have a special skill-showing assembly later in the term. That will give children an achievable ambition: 'If you practise we can all admire your efforts.'

We all have showing assemblies for classwork, and it can help if we have celebration assemblies for all kinds of improved skills. For example diligent effort resulting in improvement at painting Warhammer® models, doing bike stunts in the playground and cataloguing bizarre collections, as well as the more usual sport, music, dance and drama can all be admired.

The aim is to celebrate the children's learning to develop patient diligence.

Bible verse

Proverbs 21, v5 (New King James).

The plans of the diligent lead surely to plenty,
But those of everyone who is hasty, surely to poverty.

Prayer

Dear Lord, you have given us so many skills. We know how important it is to make a big effort to use these skills. Help us to work patiently and diligently so that we don't waste the talents you have given us. Amen

Thought for the day

Let us remember that in whatever we do we have to work slowly, steadily and with patience and tireless persistence.

If life gives you scraps – make quilts

Theme

Making the very best of whatever life throws at us.

Preparation

What you need for this assembly is rather specific.

You will need a bag of old clothes or old pieces of material. If you have had a jumble sale, you may have some old clothes in a cupboard. If not, you may have some scraps of material somewhere in the school.

You also need an item of patchwork. If you ask in the staffroom the week before you plan to do the assembly, you will almost certainly find someone who has a patchwork bag, cushion cover or, best of all, quilt.

Before you begin, put the item of patchwork (hereafter called 'the quilt') in the bottom of a bag. It's for the grand finale. On top, stuff all the old clothes or bits of material. Put the bag by your feet.

The assembly

Tell the story of the disappointing day. Whenever you come to a part of the story where you experience a disappointment, pull out an item of clothing or scrap of fabric and rip it. You will almost certainly need a pair of scissors to get each rip started; you might want to do this in advance. Then cast it away from you in disappointment and disgust. Throw it down by your feet.

My mother *(or friend, sister, aunt, long-lost cousin from Waingapu, whoever you choose)* came to visit last weekend. I was so looking forward to seeing her.

I planned that in the morning I would pick her up from the station at a quarter to ten, and then we would go to *(name the prettiest local town)* and have coffee and chocolate cake in a tearoom.

Then we would look around the shops. I wanted to visit a bookshop and browse as I needed a new book to read. After that I planned that we would go to my favourite fish restaurant for lunch. Next we would come home, sit in the garden and chat.

At half past four we would have a cup of tea and a piece of cake in the garden.

In the evening I planned that we would go out to the cinema for the six o'clock showing of *(name a popular current film)*.

After that we would go to a really nice pub, have some supper and a drink, then come home for a cup of hot chocolate, watch the news and go to bed.

I thought this would all be perfect.

But it didn't work out quite as I had planned.

First of all, her train was late and so there wasn't time for a cup of coffee and a piece of cake as well as going shopping. So *(pick up a piece of cloth and rip it in anger)* that was spoiled. *(Throw it on the floor by your feet.)*

Then, when my mother got off the train she said she had a bad cold and didn't want to go trailing around the shops. So *(pick up a piece of cloth and rip it in anger)* that was spoiled. *(Throw it on the floor by your feet.)*

Then when I suggested we just go to the bookshop, she told me she had forgotten her glasses and wouldn't be able to look at any of the books. So *(pick up a piece of cloth and rip it in anger)* that was spoiled. *(Throw it on the floor by your feet.)*

When I suggested we should pick up a take-away from my favourite fish restaurant and take it home, she said she had gone off fish. So *(pick up a piece of cloth and rip it in anger)* that was spoiled. *(Throw it on the floor by your feet.)*

I was just about to suggest we went home and had a sandwich in the garden when it started to rain. So *(pick up a piece of cloth and rip it in anger)* that was spoiled. *(Throw it on the floor by your feet.)*

I realised that as she did not have her glasses we would not be able to go to the cinema later. So *(pick up a piece of cloth and rip it in anger)* that was spoiled. *(Throw it on the floor by your feet.)*

And as she did not feel well enough to shop she wouldn't want to go out in the evening to a pub. So *(pick up a piece of cloth and rip it in anger)* that was spoiled. *(Throw it on the floor by your feet.)*

I realised that all my plans were, like these pieces of cloth, in complete ruins. I felt like getting really cross and fed up.

But I thought: I don't see my mother very often. And, besides, it would be very bad manners as well as unkind to be so impatient as to lose my temper just because things were not going to work out as I had planned.

So I had a little think.

We didn't do the shopping, but we did go to the tearoom and had a cup of coffee and some cake. *(Put a piece of cloth back in the bag.)*

After happily chatting for half an hour, I left my mother enjoying her cake. I ran over to the bookshop and bought an audio tape of her favourite BBC comedy programme. *(Put a piece of cloth back in the bag).*

Then I put her in the car, wrapped a cosy rug round her legs and drove home the pretty way. *(Put a piece of cloth back in the bag.)*

She liked seeing *(name local beauty spot, interesting village, old castle, splendid view, pretty river, whatever)*, which she enjoyed whilst sitting warm in the car with the rug round her. *(Put a piece of cloth back in the bag.)*

When we got home we had soup and sandwiches in the kitchen, then I lit the fire. We sat together and had a cup of tea and a good natter. And she had a little sleep. *(Put a piece of cloth back in the bag).*

At six o'clock I telephoned for a pizza. We ate that and then sat back by the fire. She couldn't see the TV as she had forgotten her glasses, but she enjoyed listening to the tape of her favourite comedy programme. *(Put a piece of cloth back in the bag.)*

At nine o'clock we listened to a radio play and at ten we had a cup of hot chocolate and listened to the news.

On our way up to bed my mother said she felt much better and that it had been one of the nicest days she could remember. *(Put a piece of cloth back in the bag.)*

Now, the reason I am telling you all of this is because at one point all of my hopes for the day lay in rags. I was very disappointed indeed. I felt like getting really cross and stamping my foot.

But I didn't. Instead I decided to be patient about events and make the best of the day. I tried to be creative and work with what was still possible.

Some people do that with old rags like these. Some people are clever with their hands and can turn old scraps *(indicate the bag)* into something very beautiful.

Like this. *(Pull out the quilt, or whatever.)*

Today's assembly is on...

If you are to make this from old rags you have to be a bit clever. It takes imagination, patience, time and care.

It's just the same with our lives. When things go wrong it is easy to get cross and fed up. We can be hasty and bad tempered and strop off.

Then all we are left with is the rags – the disappointment and frustration.

If we are a bit clever about life we can use what it does give us and make something good out of it.

Like quilt making, it takes patience, imagination, time and care.

Let's never forget that sometimes life gives us scraps – but if we want to, we can always make quilts.

Bible verses

2 Corinthians 4, v7–10 (CEV).

The real power comes from God and not from us. We often suffer, but we are never crushed. Even when we don't know what to do, we never give up. In times of trouble, God is with us, and when we are knocked down, we get up again.

Prayer

Dear Lord, you know that sometimes our life is not quite as we would choose it to be. Please help us have the patience and the will to make the best of what we have. With your help our life can be a great one. Amen

Thought for the day

If life gives you scraps – make quilts.

I'll get by with a little help from my friend

Theme

We can often get a great deal more out of life if we co-operate rather than compete.

Preparation

You will need four lengths of 7.5 cm (3 inch) drainpipe, the length depending upon the length of the children's arms (about 2½ to 3 metres/8 to 10 feet in all). Each length should be long enough to cover a child's arm from underarm to wrist. The pipe is quite cheap, and is available from builder's merchants. Before the assembly measure the length of two selected children's arms and cut the pipes to fit shoulder to wrist. They can slide on over school jumpers.

You also need:
- a large bar of chocolate or a box of wrapped chocolates – Fairtrade chocolate is, of course, ideal (notice how much chocolate is featured in this book);
- some gaffer tape or tape strong enough to support the pipe on the child's arm;
- two children – choose two who are good sports and also competitive.

The assembly

This assembly is based on an ancient story about heaven and hell. You need to play it as a sporting challenge.

Now, I have here a large plate of chocolate and I am going to let two lucky children eat it!

But they have to win it. This is what they have to do.

Call out one child. Slide two of the pipes over the child's arms and secure the pipes with the tape. Put the chocolate on the table in front of the child.

Now this is called the Chocolate Challenge. You can eat as much chocolate as you like but you must eat it with fingers. (*Make very sure you don't say '**your** fingers'.*) You can't just scoff it off the table! You have four minutes to get the chocolate off the table and eat it.

Go!

The child will probably try throwing the chocolate up in the air and catching it in their mouth. Commentate as if it were a sport – get the crowd excited!

After a good four minutes of loopy clowning, and not much – if any – chocolate consumption, stop the proceedings and ask out another child.

Well, they are not doing too brilliantly. Would you . . . like to try?

Strap the drainpipes onto the second child's arms.

Right, now there are two people taking the Chocolate Challenge. Go!

More fevered commentating along the lines of 'And they've got the chocolate in the air. That was a terrific throw. Oh no! They've dropped it again! Here comes another attempt. Will this be the one . . .'

Now, you may have hit upon a child who immediately sees that this is a task that demands team work. In that case you can go straight on to the chat. If not, then you will have two children who are attempting to throw chocolate in the air and catch it in their mouths. Let this run for about four or five minutes, keeping up the idea of a competition. Then continue.

Well, no one seems to be winning here.

How else might you manage to get to eat the chocolate?

Hopefully, either the children themselves or some of their friends will realise that the only way to get to eat the chocolate involves helping each other.

They must feed each other the chocolate.

At this point pause for huge congratulations, claps and chocolate consumption. If a child in the audience realised that they had to feed each other chocolate, then give that child some to eat. Virtue need not always be its own reward.

Well, two children have succeeded in taking and winning the Chocolate Challenge.

How did they do it?

Take answers.

What did it show us?

Take answers and suggestions.

It showed us that if we want to win a prize that we really value, we do not always have to try to beat someone else.

Sometimes it's co-operation, not competition, that will help you succeed.

Bible verses

Ecclesiastes 4, v9–12 (Good News Bible).
Two are better than one, because together they can work more effectively. If one of them falls down, the other can help him up. But if someone is alone and falls, it's just too bad, because there is no one to help him. Two people can resist an attack that would defeat one person alone. A rope made of three cords is hard to break.

Prayer

Dear Lord, help us to remember that sometimes it's co-operation, not competition, that will help us to succeed. We ask you to be always with us, reminding us to work together and help each other. Amen

Thought for the day

If one could be made to understand that caring only for oneself is bondage while feeding others is freedom, then life would be easy for all.
Shantanand Saraswati, quoted in Inspirational Thoughts *by Tycho Photiou*

Getting the picture at lunchtime

Theme

'All things are created twice, once in the imagination, then in reality' (Steven R. Covey). First we imagine what a really good lunchtime would look like – then we work out how to make it happen.

Preparation

This is one of those 'keep them guessing' assemblies. The point is to show the children that we have to know what we are aiming for in the playground if we are to achieve it.

It is no good just hoping that the playtimes will be wonderful if they do not have a clear image in their heads of what 'wonderful' looks like. Just as you can't put a jigsaw together if you don't know what is on the picture on the box, you can't put a happy playground together if you haven't got a clear image of a happy playground. You need a picture in your head to work towards.

This assembly requires a good deal of organising in advance – but if you are having a big push on lunchtimes it is worth the effort.

You will need to read all of these instructions through first. It's actually a very simple assembly, designed to be easily understood by both Key Stages 1 and 2.

Ideally you need a digital camera. If you don't have one, it is worth considering having a quiz night to raise money for one. They are fantastically useful as they present the children with images of themselves and their school life very quickly, in a huge range of formats.

You will need to go into the playground and set up some shots of a happy playtime. These need to be staged because you want a photograph of exactly what you would like to see in the playground.

These are some ideas for the photographs:

- Children turning a rope and skipping.
- Children playing games such as jacks/fivestones/marbles.
- Children queuing patiently by the climbing bars/climbing frame/ slide/adventure equipment or whatever big structure you may have.
- Children playing co-operatively with cars.
- Children sharing and helping each other off and on the bikes (even the red bike!).
- Children happily playing football.
- Children playing two-ball.
- Any other games or activities your school may have.

Aim for about ten photographs.

If you don't have much for the children to do at playtime, you can take photographs of them playing together happily. However, you might like to consider more activities and equipment at lunchtime.

Now you need to print off two copies of each of the photographs.

Keep one set aside. If you can afford it, it would be good to laminate this set.

Take the other set. Without muddling up the photographs, cut each into about thirty unevenly shaped pieces, in the manner of a simple jigsaw.

You will not be expecting children to put the jigsaws together. In fact, if they can, the entire assembly will fall apart!

Now get an envelope for each cut-up photograph. Put one photograph into each envelope.

Have ready in the assembly area a large display board. Perhaps you could borrow a mobile one from a classroom for the duration of the assembly.

Keep the whole pictures of the playground out of sight.

You will also need a standard jigsaw in a box.

The assembly

I need volunteers for a difficult job.

Call out ten children of assorted ages.

Now, I have here ten jigsaw puzzles. I am going to give you one each and I want you to tip them out onto the floor and put them together.

Do this.

Off you go.

Do a bit of commentating along the lines of the following.

You seem to be having some difficulty.

Come on, what's the problem?

There are only thirty pieces.

Hurry up, let's get them finished.

Why haven't you got them all right yet?

Why can't you do it?

After a few minutes of, hopefully, fairly hapless endeavour, stop them.

Is there something you need before you can put a jigsaw together?

Yes?

What?

With luck someone, either in the audience or on the stage, will say 'You need a picture to follow.' or words to that effect.

You are quite right. You need the picture on the box.

Hold up the standard jigsaw.

This is a 1,000 *(or whatever)* piece jigsaw and you would never think of trying to put it together without the picture on the box.

Well, as it happens I do have the pictures for these jigsaws.

Take the complete photographs out one by one and hold them up. Say what they are, for example:

This one is a picture of Katie, Aisha, Sophie and Lotte all skipping.

This is one of twenty boys playing football without arguing.

Now if I asked my volunteers to put the jigsaws together and gave them these uncut photographs and enough time, they would be able to do it. That is because they would know what they were aiming for. They would have a clear picture in their heads of what they were trying to create.

Now what is all of this about? Why am I fiddling about with pictures of the playground and jigsaws?

Because I want you to make the playground a better place, and I think it would help if you could see what I am aiming for.

I want the playground to look like this.

Hold each picture up one at a time, describe what it is and say why it's desirable, for example:

This picture is of Aisha, Katie, Sophie and Lotte skipping. They are taking turns with the rope and they are waiting patiently for their go. They are sharing the game without arguing. This is the behaviour we are looking for.

Go through all the photographs, talking about the desirability of the behaviour shown. Pin each uncut picture up on the display board after you explain what it shows.

So let's go back to the jigsaws.

We could not do the jigsaws without a picture to guide us.

We needed to see the picture so we could understand what we were trying to do.

It's the same with the playground.

We need to have a clear picture in our heads of exactly what we want the playground to look like so we have something to aim for.

This is what we want.

Point to the photographs.

Let's see if we can do it.

Optional follow-up

I am going to make a big display of these pictures on a noticeboard.

We are going to try to add to it lots of new photographs for us to copy – showing lots of other really good playground behaviour.

Whenever you see behaviour like this *(point to photographs)* outside, I want you to notice who was doing it, write their names on a slip of paper, and we'll pin it next to the picture.

If you do things you see in the pictures, you can add your own name.

Let's see how many names we can get on the noticeboard by the end of the week.

Next week, in assembly, we will call some people out to the front to talk about how they managed to follow the pictures.

Bible verses

Proverbs 16, v3, 7 (Good News Bible).
Ask God to bless your plans, and you will be successful in carrying them out. When you please the Lord, you can make your enemies into friends.

Prayer

Dear God, you gave us Jesus to be the picture on the box. We are supposed to try to be like him. That is not easy, so please will you help us. Please help us to see when we can do the right things, and steer us away from doing wrong things. Amen

Thought for the day

First, let us imagine a good way of living.
Second, let us work very hard together to make it happen.

Joy goes on *Blind Date*

Theme

It's often not what you get, but what you give that brings you greatest happiness.

Preparation

This is a good emergency assembly – it needs almost no preparation other than photocopying the script five times so that each actor has one. There is no need for the actors to learn any words. They obviously read from an autocue on the real *Blind Date*.

You will need:
◆ a screen or display board to hide the dater from the datees;
◆ a quick rehearsal if possible – it will probably help.

The assembly

First, you will need to choose three children or members of staff to be the three boys behind the screen. You have to have boys because the girl must be called Joy. You could have three female teachers or girls, but they would have to dress up as boys.

Then you need a girl to sit with you, on the dater side of the screen.

All of this will probably be familiar to even your youngest child.

You: Good morning, everybody, and welcome to *Blind Date*. (*Get them to give a cheer, but stop them fairly quickly – you need enthusiasm without riot.*) We have a lovely girl here tonight who is looking for Mr Right. Her name is Joy. Give Joy a clap.

(*Encourage enthusiastic clapping – even the odd whistle is fine.*)

Now, Joy is quite an unusual name. Who knows what the word 'joy' means?

Take a couple of answers until you get them to realise that 'joy' means deep happiness.

That's right, 'joy' means real, deep happiness.

We also have three splendid chaps on the other side of the screen. Give a wave to the audience, chaps. Well done! And you can all give these brave chaps a big cheer.

Encourage more cheering – you want the children to be completely involved in the action. Before you start you need to dispatch any miserable members of staff who might try to hush the children off to a wonderful 'extra planning time' opportunity!

Now, Joy, you can ask these three chaps five questions each. Then you have to choose the lucky one. I wonder which one is going to be the lucky person who gets to go out with Joy!

Right, let's meet our three contestants who are going to play *Blind Date!*

Contestant number 1, can you please tell us your name?

Number 1: My name is Mr Takealot *(pronounced 'take a lot')*.

Contestant number 2, can you please tell us your name?

Number 2: My name is Mr Keepalot *(pronounced 'keep a lot')*.

Contestant number 3, can you please tell us your name?

Number 3: My name is Mr Givealot *(pronounced 'give a lot')*.

Thank you very much, that's wonderful. Now, Joy, have you got your questions ready? Good, now who are you going to ask first?

Joy: Mr Takealot. Mr Takealot, where do you like to go on a Friday evening?

Mr Takealot: Well, I like to go to a bar full of celebrities and then on to a club.

Joy smiles.

Joy: Mr Keepalot?

Mr Keepalot: I like to go to the opera, and then on to an expensive restaurant.

Joy smiles.

Joy: Mr Givealot?

Mr Givealot: I go into London and help deliver soup to the homeless.

Joy looks surprised.

Next question.

Joy: Mr Keepalot, what sort of car do you drive?

Mr Keepalot: I drive a BMW 7 series.

Joy smiles.

Joy: Mr Takealot?

Mr Takealot: I drive a Ferrari Testarossa.

Joy smiles.

Joy: Mr Givealot?

Mr Givealot: I ride a bike.

Joy looks surprised again.

Joy: Mr Takealot, if you could travel anywhere in the world, where would you go?

Mr Takealot: I'd go to a hot country. But the hotel would have to have a big fence all round it because I wouldn't want to be bothered by poor people.

Joy looks a little worried.

Joy: Mr Keepalot?

Mr Keepalot: Well, I'd go off in my yacht. I'd sail wherever I wanted to go. I like my yacht as I can do as I want and I don't have to think about anybody but myself.

Joy looks anxious.

Joy: Mr Givealot?

Mr Givealot: I usually share a big house near the sea with lots of friends. We don't have much money but we usually have lots of fun!

Joy smiles.

Joy: If I were ill, how would you treat me, Mr Takealot?

Mr Takealot: I wouldn't treat you any way as I wouldn't come near you! I hate ill people, they are sooo boring.

Joy looks shocked.

Joy: Mr Keepalot?

Mr Keepalot: I wouldn't go near you either. I might catch something!

Joy looks shocked.

Joy: Mr Givealot?

Mr Givealot: I would visit you. I would bring you something good to eat and some flowers, and I would read your favourite book to you and make you laugh a lot.

Joy looks pleased.

Joy: Mr Takealot, if you had only £5 left in the world, what would you do with it?

Mr Takealot: I'd buy myself a fancy cocktail.

Joy looks unimpressed.

Joy: Mr Keepalot?

Mr Keepalot: I would keep it secret and spend it slowly on little treats for me.

Joy looks shocked.

Joy: Mr Givealot?

Mr Givealot: I'd share it with you.

Joy beams.

Well, Joy, who is it to be?

Mr Takealot, who likes to go to smart bars full of celebrities, drives a Ferrari Testarossa and holidays in hot countries.

Or Mr Keepalot, who likes the opera and fancy restaurants, drives a BMW 7 series and holidays on his yacht.

Or Mr Givealot, who rides a bike, helps feed hungry people; who would look after you if you were poorly, and would happily share his last £5 with you.

Joy: No contest. Mr Givealot. Maybe I won't have fast cars and a smart lifestyle, but I'll have everything that really matters in life.

Well done, Mr Givealot! Joy has chosen you! *(Encourage wild applause!)*

That's clear then. If you take a lot or try to keep a lot, you won't get to know joy. If you give a lot then you can be pretty sure joy will be yours.

So if we want to know joy – that is real happiness – we had better remember to be the sort of people who give a lot. Like Mr Givealot, we must think of others before ourselves. Mr Givealot helps poor and homeless people, he'd look after

Joy if she were ill, and he likes to share his time and his money with other people. That's the way to find joy!

Now I want you all to go away and spend time this week thinking about how you could be like Mr Givealot. I want real suggestions.

Perhaps you can think about this in your circle times.

I want you to put your ideas up on the assembly noticeboard and we will look at them next week. We will try out the best ideas.

So *(in true TV show style)*, let's hear it one last time for this week's successful *Blind Date* contestant . . . Mr Givealot! *(Encourage more applause.)*

Thank all the contestants and invite a round of applause.

If we are going to try to be like Mr Givealot this week, perhaps we'd better get a bit of help first. So let's ask God to give us a hand as we try to think of others.

Bible verses

Matthew 22, v37–40 (NIV).
Jesus replied: 'Love the Lord your God with all your heart and with all your soul and with all your mind.' This is the first and greatest commandment. And the second is like it: 'Love your neighbour as yourself.' All the Law and the Prophets hang on these two commandments.'

Prayer

Dear Lord, we want to look after each other. Please help us to see opportunities for caring for each other. Inspire us with ideas so that we find ways to put others before ourselves and learn to help them. Amen

Thought for the day

Do all the good you can,
By all the means you can,
In all the ways you can,
In all the places you can,
At all the times you can,
To all the people you can,
As long as ever you can.
John Wesley

Lesson from fishing 1

Theme

Life may put some serious temptations in our way and we must learn how to spot them and then avoid them.

Preparation

You will need:

- a couple of shiny coloured sweet wrappers;
- little bits of bait-sized pieces of bread;
- a reel of cotton or, better still, a reel of fishing line;
- five long sticks or broom handles;
- a bottle of alcopop (optional).

A couple of small plastic insects are useful, but only if you can find them easily. Don't be tempted to use anything real. The front rows will be so transfixed by the wriggling worm or whatever that they will take in nothing of the assembly. Also they will shriek – a lot.

The assembly

Cast

Several children to be fish swimming around in an imaginary pond, and five children to be anglers on the bank.

The action

Ask the children to pretend to swim about, and the others to sit with their rods and lines.

Look at all these beautiful fish swimming around in the pond. This pond is where they live. It's like their town and they think they are safe there. But they are not quite as safe as they think.

Here on the bank are some anglers who want to catch the fish. They are very clever anglers. They are using all sorts of bait to catch the fish. They have to make their hooks look as tempting as possible. Look *(use the children's real names)*, Sarah is using a shiny wrapper, Anish is using a piece of bread that will look tasty to a fish and Ranjeet has a beautiful ladybird.

The fish are swimming around and they are very tempted by these wriggly, shiny, beautiful-looking things. But if they bite them they will be caught and they might end up as someone's dinner!

Some fish live to be very old because they are very careful. They don't swim along with the shoals of little fish all chasing the first tempting, shiny thing that comes their way. They are cautious and unless they are sure they see something real to eat they stay well away. They know that you have to be careful if you want to stay safe.

Stop the action and tell the audience to give the actors a big clap. Have them sit down where they are while you go on with the assembly.

Our life can be like that. Children meet all sorts of dangers and temptations.

Those are often carefully disguised so they look safe when they are not. Biscuits, sweets and even drinks can look lovely and be very tempting but too many will make us fat or even ill.

Ask the children for some examples of wonderful packaging at this point.

Others are difficult to spot. They come wrapped up so they look like something safe when they are really very dangerous.

It is a good idea to mention alcopops at this point. You could even show them a bottle.

Sometimes people try to catch us on their hook by telling us that the really cool people try out some things. They try to catch us by saying we will be cool too if we join them. These things are often dangerous. Have you any ideas about what they might be?

Answers might include smoking, getting drunk, petty theft, and drug taking.

Never forget the fish that get caught. Things that look attractive may have hidden dangers. Be careful about what you try.

Be very careful not to follow the crowd.

Be like the careful, wise fish who thinks first, stays away from the tempting shiny things, doesn't follow the crowd and doesn't get caught.

Bible verses

Proverbs 3, v21, 23 (Good News Bible).
Hold on to wisdom and insight, my son. Never let them get away
from you.
You can go safely on your way and never even stumble.

Proverbs 1, v10, 15 (Good News Bible).
When sinners tempt you, my son, don't give in.
Don't go wth people like that, my son. Stay away from them.

Prayer

Dear God, give us the wisdom to recognise dangerous things when they
come near us. Give us the strength to stay away from them. Amen

Thought for the day

Let us always remember that things that look attractive may have hidden
dangers. Let us remember to be careful about what we try. Let us never do
anything just because we want to look cool.

Once upon a time

Theme

Our actions speak much, much louder than our words.

Preparation

You will need:

◆ a pen;
◆ a pad of Post-it notes.

You will also need a member of staff to help you – let them read this through before the assembly to give them time to get into the part. Do not use the name Eric if a child attending the assembly has it; choose something no one has. It could be a girl's name.

The assembly

Once upon a time there was a boy called Eric. This boy, in fact. *(Indicate the teacher standing next to you.)*

This is Eric and this is his story.

As Eric goes about his day you follow him around. Eric provides a running commentary upon his actions and behaviour and you write those comments on Post-it notes – I advise just one or two words, enough to act as an aide-mémoire. When each Post-it is written on, silently stick it on the floor by the place he carried out the action.

Eric won't want to be reading this script during the assembly, so he will need to have some ideas before he starts. He will be able to think up plenty of examples. This can be hammed up, but don't forget that Eric is an awful character. He should not be cute. We are not looking at Just William.

Eric: I hate getting up in the morning. I can't be bothered. *(You write note, e.g. 'Eric is lazy', and stick it on the floor.)* Oh, listen to my mum going on and on. I don't care, I'm not getting up yet. *(You write note, e.g. 'Is rude to mother', and stick it on the floor.)*

I may as well get up, but I won't wash or clean my teeth. *(Note: 'Is dirty')*

I'm just going to put my school clothes on and go to school. I won't look for my bag, and I can't be bothered to find my pencil. I'll cadge one at school. *(Note: 'Disorganised').*

Carry on in this vein. He goes to school; he might stop for a bit of shoplifting on the way. It is late when he gets to school but he doesn't care. He's rude to his teacher. He bullies another child into lending him a pencil, he nicks someone's crisps at break. He does awful things all day.

Do this for about four or five minutes, then ask Eric to stop and sit down at the side of the room. Now you talk to the school.

That was Eric. Did you know that he has been telling us a very interesting story? No? Well, he has. He left us clues about his story wherever he went. It is the story of Eric. Shall I tell you his story? It goes like this.

Now go around the area, picking up the Post-its and turning them into sentences that tell Eric's story.

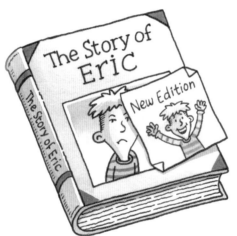

Eric was not a very nice boy. He had some horrible habits. Like laziness, and being rude to his mother when she tried to get him up for school in the morning. He wasn't a very clean boy either; he didn't wash and he didn't clean his teeth.

Continue until you have picked up all of the Post-its and improvised the story, using all of the notes.

Eric didn't know it, but he was telling us his story all day long. It wasn't a very nice story, was it? If we had asked Eric to tell us his story he wouldn't have told us this one. He probably would have told us that he was OK, that he was good at football and had lots of friends.

The trouble is that our lives tell our real story for us. Actions really do speak louder than words.

Now, let's go back and see if Eric can try to write another story of his life.

Now go through the whole procedure again. (That's why I said take just four or five minutes for the first version.) This time Eric makes different choices, behaving in an exemplary manner.

Now, let's read the new story of Eric.

Again, pick up Post-its, turning them into sentences as you go.

Make this story sound attractive and upbeat.

That was a better story, wasn't it? How did Eric make his life a better story?

He made different choices. This time he chose to do better things.

He thought about other people's feelings and happiness and he put those first.

What story do you want told about you? Make sure the story of your life is the one you would want to be told. The only way to do this is to be careful about the things you do and the things you say, for they are the plotlines you leave along the way.

Get the school to give your assistant a big clap.

Bible verses

Matthew 12, v33–5 (CEV).
A good tree produces only good fruit, and a bad tree produces bad fruit. You can tell what a tree is like by the fruit it produces . . . Your words show what is in your heart. Good people bring good things out of their hearts, but evil people bring evil things out of their hearts.

Prayer

Dear Lord, you gave us the way to live. Your story is the Gospel, the Good News. Help us to be good news too. Help us to live as you would like us to live and to tell a good news story to all the people we meet on our way through life. Amen

Thought for the day

If our lives are an open book, let's make it a good read.

The emotional environmentalist

Theme

To show the children that, as a school, we aim to put good feelings of being loved and cared for inside them and, in addition, to immerse them in an environment of love and care.

Preparation

You will need two Tupperware-type boxes. Both must have well-fitting lids. One must fit completely inside the other; if possible, have one considerably larger than the other. Ideally, you will be able to shake the sealed small one around inside the sealed larger one.

If you happen to have a transportable fish in school (the goldfish type, not a piece of battered haddock), you could bring that to the assembly.

You could also bring a pot plant – or any old plant, so long as it's alive and still has its roots.

You will need to photocopy two sets of the words below. Cut up each set into separate slips, put one set into an envelope marked 'Inside' and the other into an envelope marked 'Outside'.

Feel appreciated.	We notice you getting things right.
Don't feel stupid.	We are honest with you.
Feel in charge of your life.	We forgive you.
We are kind.	We encourage sharing.
We listen.	

Permission to Photocopy

The assembly

This assembly is unlike many of the other assemblies, in that it is not designed to encourage the children to strive to great heights of goodness.

The point of this assembly is to show the children that their school has thought carefully about creating a caring environment. The children are fortunate to be able to live and grow in it.

First, it aims to show the children that you need certain things if you are to flourish:
- *A fish in water, but with no gills, is a dead fish.*
- *A plant with no water in its stem and leaves will wilt and die.*
- *A person who does not feel safe, respected, approved of, appreciated, loved and cared for will not flourish.*

Secondly, we need to immerse the children in a healthy, emotionally nourishing environment, replete with the right things, so they may grow to be their best selves:
- *Put a fish in polluted water and it will die.*
- *Put a plant in the dark or feed it with contaminated water and it will die.*
- *Put a child in a cold, uncaring, violent or cynical environment and their best self will die.*

What does the word 'environment' mean? *(Take answers.)*

That's right, it means the habitat in which you live.

If you were a fish, what kind of environment would you need to live and thrive? *(Take answers.)*

Yes, you would need water. You would need water all around you and you would need water to go through your gills. Without water you would die.

If you have brought a fish you could point out how much the fish would dislike going outside to play football, how uncomfortable it would be in assembly sitting on the floor, how it wouldn't thank you for a trip to McDonald's and so on.

It's the same with plants. If I want this plant to live, and maybe even look a little healthier, I need to make sure it has the right environment. What does a plant need?

(Take answers.)

Yes, it needs light, good soil, the right temperature. It also needs water, to take up through its roots and flow around through its stem and leaves. No water inside the plant means a wilted, then dead plant.

Depending upon the age of the children, you can ask them a couple of questions about plant structure and so on.

What about us? *(Get a child up to the front. Let's call them Joe.)*

What does Joe need? *(Take polite answers.)*

That's right. Joe needs water, food and oxygen. He needs oxygen all around him and he needs oxygen inside him. If he doesn't have oxygen in the air he breathes, he will die. If he doesn't have oxygen in his blood, he will die. His brain will die. *(Be prepared for hecklers at this point: 'How could you tell, Miss?' 'What would be the difference?' A reply such as 'Even Joe wouldn't still be grinning.' should be enough.)* We need to have good things inside us and we need to have good things around us.

Thank Joe politely, ask everyone to give him a clap, and send him back to his place.

But we need other things, inside us and all around us, as well.

We need to feel that we matter. We need to feel that people like us. We need to feel that we are capable. We need to feel that we can be in control of ourselves and our lives, and are always able to be our best selves. Imagine it like this.

Take the small plastic box and remove the lid. Have ready the envelope of slips marked 'Inside'. You will need to display each slip so the children can see it.

Imagine this box is you. Because we know you need good things to enable you to grow, we try really hard to put these things inside you.

So we try to make sure you feel appreciated *(put slip in the box)*.
We don't want you ever to feel stupid *(put slip in the box)*.
We want to help you be in charge of your life *(put slip in the box)*.
We try to be kind to you *(put slip in the box)*.
We listen to you *(put slip in the box)*.
We always try to notice you getting things right *(put slip in the box)*.
We are honest with you *(put slip in the box)*.
We forgive you *(put slip in the box)*.
We try to share with you *(put slip in the box)*.

These things are important. We want you to have them inside you.

Put the lid firmly onto the little box with all the slips secured inside. Now get the big plastic box.

This box is our school. You spend a great deal of time here in school.

Put the little box into the big box. Leave the lid off the big box. Have the envelope of words marked 'outside' ready.

We know it is important to put these things into our school. We try to make sure that our school values and appreciates everyone *(put slip in the box)*.

No one is allowed to make anyone else feel stupid *(put slip in the box)*.

We try to help everyone to be in charge of their life *(put slip in the box)*.

We believe it is important that everyone is kind to others *(put slip in the box)*.

We make sure we listen to you and we teach you to listen to each other *(put slip in the box)*.

We believe it is important to notice each other getting things right and not keep trying to catch each other getting things wrong *(put slip in the box)*.

We believe everyone should be honest with each other *(put slip in the box)*.

We believe forgiveness is very important *(put slip in the box)*.

We teach everyone to share *(put slip in the box)*.

These things are important. We want to have them in our school.

Put the lid on the big box. You now have the little box safe inside the big box.

Remember the fish? How it was safe in the water, with water inside its gills and water all around it?

Remember the plant? It had the right environment around it and the right environment inside it.

And Joe? He had oxygen all around him and oxygen inside him.

Well, now imagine you are the little box and the school is the big box.

You have good things inside you and good things all around you.

In this school you are in a good environment for growth!

You can make a wall display of this during the next week. You could ask classes to think of things that we need inside us and outside us in their circle times during the following week. They could add their ideas to the wall display.

Bible verses

Colossians 3, v11–14 (CEV).

Christ lives in all of us.
God loves you and has chosen you as his own special people. So be gentle, kind, humble, meek, and patient. Put up with each other, and forgive anyone who does you wrong, just as Christ has forgiven you. Love is more important than anything else. It is what ties everything completely together.

Prayer

Dear God, help us to remember that with your goodness in our hearts and your goodness all around us, we will always be safe in your loving care. Amen

Thought for the day

Let us all be thankful that we know how to make our school a people-friendly environment.
Let us remember to care for this environment and help each other to grow strong.

Search for the hero inside yourself

Theme

Sometimes going through life is like finding your way through a scary maze. We need each other to help us overcome problems when we meet them.

Preparation

You will need the following:

◆ A ball of string.

◆ If you have a CD with 'Search for the Hero Inside Yourself' by M People on it that would help to begin the assembly.

◆ Five A4 cards with one problem from the list below written on each.

The problems

1. All of the top year thinks you are seriously cool. The teachers think you are challenging. You love being a dude – but you also want to do well at school. Are you going to be able to manage to do well at school – and still be Mr Cool?

2. A new boy comes to your school. He is not very popular. In fact, he is a bit sad and some children tease him. You would like to be a friend but you are scared that people would label you 'sad' as well. What are you going to do? Be truthful.

3. You do not like your class teacher and you really think she does not like you very much – in fact, you feel she picks on you all the time. It's so bad you don't want to go to school. What should you do?

4. You find it very difficult to read. You decide you really want to improve, but you don't know how. What might you do?

5. You know that lots of younger children do not like playtime as it is a bit wild out there. You decide to help make the playground a better place to be. What one thing could you do to help other children enjoy playtime or lunchtime? Would you be brave enough to put your idea into practice?

The assembly

This is an assembly about being brave. There are lots of different ways of being brave:

◆ Firefighters are brave – they go into burning buildings and rescue people.
◆ Coastguards are brave when they go out into stormy seas to rescue people.
◆ Doctors who work in war zones are brave.
◆ Teachers who teach you lot are brave.

I know a story about someone who was brave. His name was Theseus and he was a character in a story from ancient Greece. This is his story.

Many thousands of years ago there was a king called Minos who lived in a huge palace on the island of Crete. Underneath this palace was a terrifying creature called the Minotaur. This creature had the head of a bull and the body of a man. Worse than that, all it ate was people!

Because the Minotaur was so scary, Minos had his friend Daedalus build an underground maze that was so complicated it was impossible to find a way out. Minos then sent the Minotaur to live in the maze or labyrinth and had a dinner of seven young people sent down to it once a year.

How do I kill the Minotaur with *this*?

Theseus was the son of King Aegeus of Athens. He thought that a boy-and-girl-eating half-man-half-bull creature was a very bad idea. Especially as most of the people it had eaten had been his friends.

He set off to kill the Minotaur before it could eat that year's rations.

Theseus sailed from Athens to Crete and on arrival he fell madly in love with Minos's daughter Ariadne. She told him that if he went into the maze he would (a) get eaten by the Minotaur, but if by a miracle he survived he would (b) never escape from the maze.

But she had a cunning plan! Being a homely girl and fond of knitting, she had a few balls of wool in her pocket. She tied the wool to the door of the labyrinth so that after he had killed the Minotaur Theseus would be able to follow the wool back to the entrance. This girl was good in a crisis.

Bravely, Theseus entered the maze. His whole life hung by a thread.

Miraculously the entire plan worked. It wasn't easy but Theseus found the Minotaur, killed it, followed the wool out of the maze, rescued the Minotaur's next meal – seven young Athenians – got the girl and set sail for home.

Sadly, things went downhill a bit after that, but that's another story. What matters is that Theseus was really brave and risked his life to rescue his friends and do what he thought was right. It was a case of 'He could do it – she could help!'

Now the good news is that we have no people-eating Minotaur in the basement of this school.

The bad news is that we do have scary things to face. Sometimes we need to be brave – and we can always do with some help.

So we are going to set off into our own labyrinth. In this maze lurk the sort of problems that attack us every day.

Now, I will need a volunteer to enter the labyrinth and face the dangers that lurk in our school.

Get a male volunteer up to the front.

I have a very long ball of wool here. I am going to tie it to *(the leg of a table, the leg of the piano, the leg of the deputy head – anything that is fairly resilient).*

I am now going to walk round and round the hall with this wool. *(Get some of the children to put their hands up, just slightly, so you can catch the wool round their hands and make it look as if the wool is going through a maze.)*

At five points along the wool line place one of the problem cards in the slightly raised hand of a child. When you have made things look a bit like a maze, go back to the front.

It was very dark in the labyrinth so I am going to blindfold our volunteer.
Do this.

Now he has to set off following the wool line until he comes to a problem.

(Move aside for him as he feels his way in the darkness.) Do a bit of commentating as he moves along the wool line. As he comes across a card, get him to stop. You read out the problem on it. Ask the whole school if they have any helpful ideas. Hopefully they will have already thought about some of the issues in their circle times. Get a member of staff to write down the ideas the children come up with.

When each of the five problems has been briefly tackled, lead the blindfolded child out of the maze and back to the front. Raise his hand in triumph.

Hooray! He is back out of the maze with some of the dangers overcome. He could do it and you could help!

You see, like Theseus and Ariadne in Crete, we have defeated some of the dangers that lurk in our school. Sometimes going through life is like finding your way through a scary maze. We need each other to help us overcome problems when we meet them.

But overcoming each of those problems requires bravery – not necessarily the same sort of bravery as a fireman or a lifeboatman, but bravery none the less. You have to be brave to ask for extra help with reading, or playing with an unpopular child, or sorting out a problem with a teacher. On those days you have to search for the hero inside yourself and defeat the scary monsters.

Thank the volunteer, get everyone to give him the usual round of applause and send him back to his place.

Bible verse

1 Chronicles 4, v10 (New King James).

Jabez called on the God of Israel saying, 'Oh, that you would bless me indeed and enlarge my territory, that your hand would be with me, and that you would keep me from evil, that I may not cause pain.' So God granted him what he requested.

Prayer

Let's ask God to help us be a hero for him, being brave and doing the right thing even when it's difficult. Let's ask him to help us to find our way through the maze of our lives.

Lord, help us to be brave enough to rescue each other. Please help us at all times. It's too hard to manage this without your help – but with you we can be heroes.

Thought for the day

Let us always try to search for the hero inside of us.

THINK before you speak

Theme

Learning to check the value of what we say before we say it: is it True, Helpful, Inspiring, Necessary, Kind?

Preparation

Oh, joy! There is almost no preparation! You just need:

◆ a flipchart and paper or a portable whiteboard – or even a painting board with some sheets of paper held onto it with Bulldog clips, if the worst comes to the worst;

◆ a blue marker pen and a red marker pen.

The assembly

Write on the board a sum, say 26 x 30.

Who can tell me the answer to this sum? Quick. It's second helpings at lunchtime *(or whatever would encourage your children)* for the first person who puts their hand up!

Take the first answer, right or wrong, and put it up as the answer.

Is that right? How do we know? Let's just check it.

Do the sum, carefully, on the board.

Is that right? How could we check it further?

You now have to follow the suggestions of the children. The aim of this part of the assembly is to demonstrate that there are lots of ways of checking our answer to see if it is right.

We could divide the answer by 10 and then by 3 and see what we got. We should have 26.

Let's try that. *(Do the sum.)*

How else could we have checked it?

Yes, we could have used a calculator. But sometimes we make mistakes on a calculator.

How could we check the calculator answer?

Do 26 + 26 thirty times? Yes. Slow, but it would help.

How many times would we have to check the answer before we had a definite idea that we were right? *(Wait for suggestions.)*

Yes, I'd say that. About two or three.

Now imagine that you have to pay me that sum in money. In pounds! Perhaps you have bought a really fancy stereo from me or are paying for three children to go on a school outing. You want to be certain that we have done the sum right, don't you? Of course, because a mistake would have serious consequences. You might give me too much money or you might end up owing me money.

Now, suppose you are writing a letter.

Perhaps you want to say thank you to someone for a present. What will happen if you don't read the letter through after you have written it?

You might make a terrible mistake!

Suppose you took your adored pet rabbit to the vet because he seemed poorly, and the next day you received this letter.

If you want to, you can write the letter up on the board.

'There is no need to worry about your rabbit any more. We have cured all of his problems. He was delicious.'

You would be a bit upset, wouldn't you?

But suppose they hadn't eaten your rabbit at all! The person who wrote the letter just failed to check it. It should have read: 'There is no need to worry about your rabbit any more, we have cured all of his problems. He was delirious.'

There's a big difference!

Checking things is always important. Sometimes we forget this when we talk to each other. We say things and we don't check them first.

We say things like this:

◆ You can't play football with us; you're rubbish at it.

◆ I'm not talking to Leanne any more because she's been saying things about me to Sasha.

◆ Amy goes to my ballet class. No one likes her.

◆ Have you sat next to Darren? He smells funny.

◆ Is that your drawing? I think your man looks silly.

◆ That's a rubbish football sticker. I've got loads of them.

◆ *(On a non-uniform day.)* Oh, my goodness! What do you think you're wearing? You are so sad. No one wears those any more.

Now all of these things are unkind and they may be untrue. They will also have caused a huge amount of unhappiness. If we want to have a happy school and be our best selves we can't just say anything we like.

But how do we know what it is OK to say and what is wrong? How can we check?

We know how to check to see if sums are right. We know how to check to see if words are right: if we are a bit unsure of the spelling we can look them up in a dictionary or spell-check them.

How are we going to check to see if what we say is all right?

We are going to THINK! We are going to T–H–I–N–K before we speak.

Write 'THINK' up on the flipchart or whatever and then write it downwards as an acrostic.

So we know how to think, we can use this as a guide. Before we say something, we can think and ask ourselves if it is:

True?

Helpful?

Inspiring?

Necessary?

Kind?

I would get the whole school to say it with me. They need to learn this. You can refer to this later, when resolving a difficult situation.

Whatever you say does not have to be all of these things, but if something is any of these:

- untrue

- unhelpful

- uninspiring

- unnecessary

- unkind

don't say it.

I would like each class to put what we have learned up on the classroom wall.

(Show the poster opposite and read out what it says.)

That should cut down on a lot of mistakes and a lot of misery!

Bible verses

Philippians 4, v8–9 (based on NIV).
Brothers and sisters, whatever is true, whatever is noble, whatever is right, whatever is pure, whatever is lovely, whatever is admirable – if anything is excellent or praiseworthy – think about such things . . . And the God of peace will be with you.

Prayer

Dear God, we can cause so much unhappiness by our words, and often when that happens we do not really mean to be unkind. Help us to remember to think before we speak. Help us to remember to engage brain before operating mouth. Amen

Thought for the day

Let us always remember to T-H-I-N-K before we speak.

Before you speak, THINK.

Is what you are about to say:

True?
Helpful?
Inspiring?
Necessary?
Kind?

If it isn't, don't say it.
THINK before you speak.

The ice fight

Theme

The importance of working out ways to guard our tongues when we are in a bad, spiteful mood.

Preparation

This is a 'you need to cover the assembly area with newspaper' assembly! As well as newspaper, you need a large bag of ice. You can make this but you should be able to buy it from a supermarket for about £1.

You will need several well-briefed teachers who are aware of the true consequences of participating in this assembly!

The assembly

This assembly is a bit wild. Use only members of staff.

Position four or five members of staff around the outside of the acting area, standing on newspaper. Arrive, carrying the bag of ice, and address the school along the following lines.

Hello, everyone. My name is Emily and I'm in Year 5. And these are my friends. They are just like your friends. They like music and clothes. Some like dancing, some like playing musical instruments, some like football, some like pets, some like Brownies, some like reading. *(Mention any other activities that the children in your school enjoy.)* They are a mixed group but they are all my friends in school.

Today I'm in a bad mood. I'm feeling fed up and cross, I don't really know why. I feel horrible inside, like I'm carrying a load of thoroughly uncomfortable ice.

*Now speak to each adult on the stage in turn from a distance. As you throw each unkind remark, throw a few pieces of ice with it. Do not throw the ice **at** the person. You merely need to throw the ice **to** them with a remark. They must catch the ice, or pick it up if they drop it. They need to hold it until you have been round the whole group; they can register the discomfort of this.*

The type of unkind remarks you make will be different for each school. In general, however, you need to say such things as the following:

- ◆ I don't want to play with you today. I'm best friends with Natalie now.
- ◆ You think you are so good at football, but you are just rubbish.
- ◆ I've changed my mind. You are not coming to my party any more.
- ◆ I can't believe you really like Gareth Gates/Will Young/Robbie Williams *(or whoever else is super-popular at the time)*. He's rubbish.
- ◆ Those shoes look like you bought them in a jumble sale.
- ◆ I'm not being mean or anything but you have got quite fat lately, haven't you?
- ◆ I heard Miss Simpson say you weren't going to get a part in the school play. She said you aren't anywhere near as good as you were last year.

After you have gone round the entire group, each of its members will have a piece of ice they will be keen to be rid of. Throw the rest of the ice away randomly. They can now all start lobbing insults at each other simultaneously and chucking their ice to others. The ice will melt rapidly. As it does, the fight should subside.

My ice has gone now. I felt better when I was throwing ice around, but now it's all gone I feel bad again. I don't think anyone is a very good friend at the moment.

The group give each other hostile looks and refuse to talk to each other. Address the school.

Do you think all of this unhappiness is my fault? *(Allow the children to respond.)*

So do I. I couldn't help it, though. I felt upset. What else could I have done?

Get all the staff to come and join in the discussion. Take suggestions from anyone, adults or children, as to what might have been the best thing to do when you felt the ice fight coming on.

Possible suggestions include these:
- ◆ Decide to go away by yourself until the ice melts and you feel better.
- ◆ Tell a kind friend that you feel awful and crotchety and need cheering up.
- ◆ Speak to a grown-up about how you feel.
- ◆ Try to guard your tongue until the ice melts.
- ◆ Distract yourself with a pleasant task, read a book, listen to some music, play football, look at a comic – or even have a sleep – until the bad mood passes.

◆ Find something to do that you know you are good at so you can enjoy the feeling of success.

◆ If you are at home, go off to your room, get it straight and then enjoy the feeling of being a bit more in control of things.

Take suggestions from the children and note them down. During the following week you could make a display of ideas to prevent an ice fight. 'Let's not have an ice fight.' could become a saying in school.

Bible verses

Proverbs 13, v2; 15, v1, 18; 16, v24, 21; 17, v14 (CEV).

These are some of the wise sayings of King Solomon:

You will be well rewarded for saying something kind,
But all some people think about is how to be cruel and mean.

A kind answer soothes angry feelings,
But harsh words stir them up.

Losing your temper causes a lot of trouble,
But staying calm settles arguments.

Kind words are like honey –
They cheer you up and make you feel strong.

And if you can speak kindly,
You can teach others.

The start of an argument is like a water leak –
So stop it before real trouble breaks out.

Prayer

Dear Lord, help us to keep our unkind words to ourselves. When we start trouble we don't have any idea where it will lead us. Often our stupid unkindness leads us into dreadful situations. Please help us keep our bad tempers and nasty words to ourselves. Amen

Thought for the day

Let us not get involved in ice fights. Let us always remember that harsh words sting.

The one about the hockey trial

Theme

Just because we are not good at something, that does not make us worthless people. We can always choose to be our best selves.

Preparation

Photocopy the script and give it to each of the participants in advance – ideally the day before. However, as this needs hardly any preparation, it is quite useful for a Monday morning 'It's my assembly. What am I going to do?' type of assembly. In that case, give the participants time to read it through while you fly about trying to find:

◆ six hockey sticks;
◆ six bibs;
◆ six or seven field markers or cones.

It is a good idea to use staff for the hockey players as they can take the abuse. You could, if yours is a small school with only one or two staff, use Year 6 pupils as well, but they would have to be very well briefed.

The assembly

Set out the assembly area with cones or markers. Staff will need to be able to do a bit of dribbling around cones, tackling each other for a ball – or even, space allowing, try to score and save goals. The more action, the better.

Announce that today is the day of the staff hockey trials. Call out the staff you have chosen by name, get them kitted up in bibs and arm each of them with a hockey stick.

Now start to put them through their paces. Have a couple do some dribbling around the cones and ask others if they can show you some tricks such as negotiating past each other, popping the ball over each other's sticks, even a bit of running with the ball. You may be lucky and have someone who is quite good at hockey – but it doesn't matter if they are all dire.

Permission to Photocopy

As you go around, or as you watch them try to do skilful tricks, make loud comments. Be very encouraging to those who are good at the game, use their names a great deal, praise their skills, point them out as examples to the hopeless ones. You can keep using such phrases as 'Good shot', 'Well played' and so on.

Just try a bit harder.

To the more hopeless ones say less. You might try deliberately forgetting their name, using the wrong name, asking them to get out of the way of the good ones, asking them to stand at the side and so on.

At the end praise the good ones extravagantly. Now line them up and interview them. Ask each in turn how well they felt they had played and how much they enjoyed the trials. Now ask the children how each of the staff members might behave during the rest of the day. The responses will be along the following lines:

- The ones who have been successful will be in good moods and they will be happy and cheerful. They may even boast about their success. Some might suggest that the successful ones would tease those who were hopeless.

- The ones who were useless, it will be suggested, will be in awful moods. They might sulk and get cross about everything throughout the day. They might be nasty to those who were successful. Or they might feel miserable and useless all day. They might feel inclined to give up on everything that they find difficult.

Now you can tell the school that you know you were really horrible to the hopeless ones. And you know that was wrong. Explain that just because you were awful and not your best self, that does not mean that any of the hockey players has to behave badly.

We have no control over how people behave towards us – but we can have complete control over how we respond to them.

Now ask the hockey players in turn how they could best behave throughout the rest of the day. Hope for answers like these from the good ones:

- ◆ Try not to boast.
- ◆ Think about how to be a good winner.
- ◆ Notice the things other people do well throughout the day.

Answers from the hopeless ones should be something like these:

- ◆ Try not sulking or getting in a bad mood.
- ◆ Try not to feel useless about other things we find difficult throughout the day.
- ◆ Make a determined effort not to take it out on others.

Get everyone to give the staff a big clap and let them go back to their seats.

Sum up

Everybody has things they find difficult or just can't do. We all have to face nasty people who make us feel even worse about ourselves.

We must remember that just because we are not good at something, that does not make us a worthless person. We can always choose to be our best selves, no matter how hard we find some things or how awful people try to make us feel about our failures.

Bible verses

1 John 1, v7–11 (NIV).

If we claim to be without sin, we deceive ourselves and the truth is not in us. If we confess our sins, he is faithful and just and will forgive us our sins and purify us from all unrighteousness. If we claim we have not sinned, we make him out to be a liar and his word has no place in us.

Prayer

Dear Lord, help us to remember that you love us whether we are good at things or bad at them. What matters to you is that we live as you ask us to live and that we love you, and each other, with all our hearts. Amen

Thought for the day

Just because you are not good at something, that doesn't make you a worthless person. Don't measure your worth by your talents or by other people's opinions.

The pleasure of a job well done

Theme

Discovering that there is often much more pleasure in doing jobs when we have worked hard and done them all by ourselves.

Preparation

You will need the following:
- Some Warhammer® models, or similar paintable model figures, some painted and some unpainted. Also if possible a model of Frodo from *The Lord of the Rings* (made by the same firm).
- A small pot of paint.
- A small brush.

An eager beaver in Year 5 or 6 may lend you all of this.

The assembly

How many of you have ever asked people to help you with things you could really do on your own, if you had just made the effort?

Well, this is the story of a boy who learnt the hard way that sometimes help is not a good idea.

There now follows a little drama. Cast: James, Mum, Dad.

Ask three senior Key Stage 2 children to learn and perform the play or brief three children to act out the play silently as you speak the commentary.

This is James. He is a good boy, but a bit lazy! He always wants to be helped. He's always saying, 'Dad, can you help me with my school project? Mum, I can't tidy my room, it's too messy. Can you help me, please?'

His mum and dad are very kind and usually give him a hand. Sometimes they end up doing almost the whole of his homework or his projects for him.

It is Friday after school. James finally saved up enough money to buy a whole new set of Warhammer® figures and now he is sitting in his room, looking at the figures. *(At this point get him to hold up a Frodo figure, if you have one.)* He is so excited! Tomorrow he will get up early and paint them!

His mum comes in to say he has to go to bed. He doesn't mind because tomorrow is Saturday and he can paint his models all day. That night just before he goes to sleep, he leaps out of bed and clears a little space on his chest of drawers for the figures, paints and equipment. Then he jumps back into bed and goes to sleep, dreaming about how wonderful his models will look when he has painted them.

At this point remove the figures and equipment and replace them with the fully painted figures.

In the morning he wakes up, jumps out of bed and rushes over to his box of models. There on his table, instead of the box of silver models, waiting to be painted, he sees all of the models lined up and already painted. He bursts into tears. 'Who did this?' he says. 'Who spoiled everything?'

His mum and dad are standing behind the door. They come in, looking shocked. 'We did,' they say. 'You always like people to do things for you. We thought you'd be pleased they are all ready to play with now.'

'No,' said James. 'You have spoiled everything. Having the models isn't the point. The best bit is making them and painting them. There is no fun in having them if you haven't painted them all yourself.' His day was ruined.

That boy discovered that getting things the easy way is not going to make him happy. Sometimes we forget this when we let people help us too much or give us things without making us save up first.

Ask the children to give you examples of when they have asked for help for things they could have done themselves. Have a brief talk about some things in school that the children could do on their own during the coming week.

Follow-up

During the following week, try to get a picture of Frodo. If you have a Frodo model, there may be one on the box. Photocopy the picture, blow it up to A3 size and pin it on to the noticeboard. Across the top write the legend: 'Frodo wouldn't have asked a relative to take the ring back for him! What have you done all by yourself this week?'

If no picture of Frodo is available try getting any picture of a hero and displaying a suitable legend, as follows:

– *Batman.* 'Batman wouldn't have asked his mum to save Gotham City. What have you done all by yourself this week?'

– *Boudicca.* 'Boudicca wouldn't have asked her dad to drive the chariot for her. What have you done all by yourself this week?'

You can use other appropriate examples instead.

Encourage the children to display examples of work they have completed alone or to write about things they have done all by themselves.

The next week in an assembly call up some of the children and ask them to talk about what they put on the board and how it felt to do something all by themselves. Make sure they receive a big clap.

Bible verses

Galations 6, v7, 9 (Good News Bible).
People will reap exactly what they sow . . . Let us never become tired of doing good, for if we do not give up, the time will come when we will reap the harvest.

Prayer

Dear Lord, you told us that we must not let ourselves be tempted into trying to get things the easy way. Help us to remember this and please encourage us when we are struggling. Amen

Thought for the day

Let us try to remember that there is often much more pleasure in jobs when we have worked hard and done them all by ourselves.

The strange-but-true New Year assembly

Theme
This world is wonderful, unexpected, exciting. Let's make the New Year not only good but unexpectedly exciting.

Preparation
We used a website to find the wacky facts in this assembly. If you don't like our facts, dig out your own. (Just type 'strange but true' in a search engine.) I wanted to reject number 3, but Dennis said that bloke teachers would like it. I was worried that he might start opening beer bottles with his eye sockets if I didn't agree. Such is collaboration. Such is marriage!

The assembly

Today is the first day of a New Year. We have no idea what is going to happen in the next twelve months. It's like a blank sheet of paper.

Now you might be thinking, 'Oh, that's not true. I know what will happen. It will be much like last year. I'll still find sums difficult.' or 'I'll still hate football.' or 'I'll still find making friends difficult.'

Well, maybe. Maybe some of those things might happen. But maybe not.

Sometimes life is stranger than you think and sometimes we can make it turn out quite differently from what we imagined. We can write some of the script for the year ahead and we can decide to make it amazing.

Here are ten things that happened in the last couple of years – or did they? I'm going to read you a list. Tell me which of these you think are true and which are false. I'll tell you the answers at the end.

1. In 2002, more Monopoly money was printed than real money.

2. It is against the law in Alaska to look at a moose from an aeroplane.

3. In one year 546 Australians were seen in hospital with injuries caused by trying to open bottles of beer with their eye sockets.

4. The Japanese have invented a robotic hair-washing machine. You stick your head in what looks like an upturned goldfish bowl and jets of soap and water wash your hair. Styling and drying features are optional extras.

5. All bats turn left when exiting a cave.

6. There are special shops in Tokyo that sell wigs for dogs.

7. Glasgow scientists discovered that listening to Billy Connolly was three times more effective than aspirin as a painkiller.

8. In 2001, there were 45,006 more girls born than boys.

9. In 2002, Germany won the world marbles championship for the second year in a row.

10. A restaurant manager picked up and swallowed a worm after a customer complained about finding it in his food. He then charged the customer for the worm, saying it was edible food.

11. Sheffield United fed their team baby food before matches.

12. A Dutchman who was cleaning his bathroom mixed many different cleaning fluids and blew up his lavatory. He had just left the room and was unhurt, but the explosion blew out every window in his flat.

13. Next year will be exactly the same as this year.

Right, now I'll tell you which ones were true and which were not true. Ready?

The only one that is not true is the last one. Isn't that amazing. The Dutchman really did blow up his lavatory!

At this point the assembly can go in two ways. You can do a fairly standard 'The future is in your hands' type of assembly. You can get them to set a few targets for the school, their classes and even themselves. You can make a display of these and they can add to them throughout the following week. You can even make a loose-leaf file of things they would like to do, one idea a page. As they achieve each thing they can write about it. This book can then be used next year to see what things have been achieved in the school.

Or, you can do all of that and add something different! Like this.

Well, those targets are really good. But why don't we add a few things that will make everyone who reads our book sit up and gasp! Let's add our own 'Strange but true' facts.

Then we can read out some of our achievements during a parents' assembly and ask them which were true and which were false and they would all be true! So what shall we have?

These are a few suggestions:

- Nursery/Reception children could learn an action song which they will perform to an audience of 200 people *(i.e. they will show it in an assembly).*

- Twenty Year 1 children could get a special mention from the lunchtime supervisors for having played games with each other, without arguing, in the space of one week!

- Year 2 children could get a letter from the Queen. *(If you write to her a reply is always received).*

- Year 3 children could become chicken farmers. *(We did this for a couple of years running, with great success. We borrowed an incubator from the science advisory teacher. We bought fertilised eggs from a children's farm – you can find any number of suppliers in the back of 'The Smallholder' magazine. We then set up the incubator and hatched the chicks. We kept the chicks for a few weeks, feeding them with special food called 'chick crumbs', and then gave them to a local children's farm.)*

- Year 4 children could write to the prime minister/a favourite children's author/an astronaut/a famous living artist/a ballet dancer or whatever. *(Choose people whose achievement is genuinely admirable and the result of years of work or study, not pop stars or transient celebrities who are famous only for being famous.)*

- Year 5 children could read 200 books over the year or learn circus skills. *(You can use string through tin cans for stilts and socks filled with dried beans for juggling; skills include cartwheels, handstands, headstands, walking on hands.)*

- Year 6 children could put on an art and textiles exhibition. *(They could choose a theme and work singly or in groups to create a collection of art/textiles/pottery/even painted glassware [from charity shops]. This could be staged as an exhibition in the entrance hall or similar space for a few days. As they are about to leave school and head off for the independence of secondary schools, they could be encouraged to work on this in lunchtimes and organise it themselves. If they see films, books, slides and so on about well-known painters, that will stimulate them – they will all want to be Jackson Pollock!)*

All or some of this is going to create an exciting 'strange but true' section for your book of the year.

Bible verses

Psalm 98, v1, 4–6 (CEV).
Sing a new song to the Lord!
He has worked miracles,
And with his own powerful arm,
He has won the victory.

Tell everyone on this earth
To sing happy songs
In praise of the Lord.
Make music for him on harps.
Play beautiful melodies!
Sound the trumpets and horns
And celebrate with joyful songs
For our Lord and King!

Prayer

Dear Lord, you have given us such an exciting world. Help us to use the imaginations you have given us to explore its possibilities. Let us never get so involved with the ordinary that we forget the wild excitement of creating the unusual. Amen

Thought for the day

This world is wonderful, unexpected and exciting. Let's enjoy it for all it's worth!

The teachers' coach trip

Theme

Learning that if we all put each other first, we can all end up winners.

Preparation

This is a simple assembly with little preparation. It will be readily understood by Key Stage 1 as well as being suitable for Key Stage 2.

You need to ask eight to ten members of staff to bring something large and unwieldy to assembly. If you do not have eight to ten members of staff, try to recruit a couple of parents to make up the number. Try not to use children as the humour of this situation is in seeing adults behaving badly.

Each of the staff needs to bring something that people would associate with them. These are some suggestions:

- A keyboard.
- A huge plastic box of bricks.
- A flipchart.
- A bike.
- A massive box of PE equipment.
- An armful of puppets or soft toys.
- A couple of story bags.
- A big beanbag.
- Assorted art equipment.
- A couple of large suitcases.

You **must** have:

- a huge box of pretend picnic food (carried by the school cook, if they are willing to join in; if not, give it to a teacher); include a few real sandwiches if possible;
- an armful of books and games.

It would be good to have:

- a guitar/shaking bells or another portable musical instrument.

You will need to put out ten chairs in two parallel lines, facing the front, with a very narrow aisle down the middle. This should look like a plane interior or a coach.

The assembly

The point of this assembly is to show the children that:

(a) we should not put ourselves first, and
(b) we often don't get what we want;

but:

*(c) if we **all** remember to put others first we can usually come up with a win/win solution.*

Keep the staff and their assorted lumber out of sight, ready to come in when called.

Today is the day of the staff coach trip. We are all going away for a couple of days. One by one they are going to get on the coach.

Call the staff in.

Here they are. It's time to get on the coach.

Pre-brief the staff as to how to get on the coach. They should:
– attempt to put their baggage on each other's seats;
– try to push past each other;
– bump into each other;
– tell each other to remove their things from the coach;
– justify their own luggage;
– denigrate each other's luggage;
– put their luggage in the aisles – and so on.

This should look like a disgraceful melée with people being totally selfish and aggressive to each other.

They should not be pretending to be children. It is important that they act as real, badly behaved adults. However, they can play this for maximum laughs.

Let the entire situation become as bad and mad as possible. Eventually, when it looks as if there will be blood on the carpet if you don't intervene, get up and arrive at the coach in the role of stern peacekeeping organiser.

Whatever is going on, this is a disgraceful carry-on. What are you all doing?

They all speak at once, press their case, shout, yell at each other, blame each other and so on.

Stop. I won't have this. Why have you put all of this stuff inside the coach?

The staff make more demands that they should be allowed to keep their things with them, that each one's need is the greatest and so on.

This is obviously never going to work. You can't all have your own way.

What else could you do in this situation? This coach does have a boot, you know.

Lead them through the following:
– Everything stays on – hopeless.
– Everything goes in the boot – is that the best way?
– Look at the items – which would it be good to have on the coach?

Agree to suggestions that it would be a good idea to keep the food, the books and

magazines and the musical instrument inside the coach, and put the rest of the stuff in the boot.

Help them organise this, then encourage everyone back onto the coach.

Delegate someone to hand round the sandwiches and pass round the magazines or books. If possible, have the musician play a well-known song and encourage everyone to join in.

Address the school.

Now look at that. When everyone was trying to think only of themselves it was terrible. Most unpleasant. But after people stopped and thought about the whole situation, putting their wants and desires aside, they found a really good solution.

This situation is much better than it was.

People are eating sandwiches, reading books and magazines and singing. Only three people got their own way and were able to keep the thing they had brought with them on the coach.

But because everyone thought about what was going to be good for the **whole group**, the whole group is much, much happier than they were when they all tried to get their own way.

This is called a win/win solution.

Now we all know they were only acting and that these adults are really very good indeed at putting the needs of others first.

Let's give them a big clap.

Dismiss the staff. Ask the children to try, all through the following week, to notice when they see people putting the needs of others first.

This gives a good opportunity to develop a school catch phrase in the coming weeks. If two people both want their own way, instead of saying, 'Well, you can't both have what you want,' you can say, 'Which idea shall we put in the boot?' It means there is nothing wrong with what you want, but it's not always possible for everyone to get their own way. It's less dismissive and therefore less likely to cause hostility.

Bible verses

Philippians 2, v2–5, 14–15 (CEV).
God's spirit makes you concerned for others. Live in harmony by showing love for one another . . . Be humble and consider others more important than yourselves. Care about them as much as you care about yourselves, and think the same way that Jesus thought . . . Do everything without grumbling or arguing . . . Try to shine like stars among the people of this world.

Prayer

Dear Jesus, in your lifetime you always put yourself second. You thought of others before yourself. It's a very difficult thing to do and we are only learning. Please be at our side all the time and give us a nudge when you see an opportunity for us to put others first. Then please help us as we try to be more selfless. Lord, this goes for all the grown-ups as well. We could all do with a bit of help sometimes. Amen

Thought for the day

Let's remember that if we all put each other first we all end up winners.

The web of kindness

Theme

Recognising that in a caring and loving school we are all caught up in a web of kindness.

This is most suited to Key Stage 1.

Preparation

All you need is a ball of wool.
You might want to use a flipchart to record the children's ideas.

The assembly

This assembly is about belonging, belonging to each other. We are all joined up to each other like parts of a spider's web. And what are we all connected by? What makes the spider's web? We are all connected to each other by kindness.

Have you ever noticed how kind this school is? Random acts of kindness, indiscriminate generosity, wholesale thoughtfulness, occur all the time.

Only this morning . . . (*Give an example of a kind act that has occurred this morning: someone fetched something for you, made an offer of help, said thank you – don't make it a big event; choose an ordinary act of kindness.*)

That was kind, wasn't it?

What kind things have happened to you recently? Let's see if we can make a list on the flipchart.

You might want to get someone to do the writing while you take answers. Ask them to summarise the suggestions. If one suggestion is repeated, put a tick or star after it. You can then say, 'My, what a lot of people have been kind to each other when they have seen a friend upset in the playground' or whatever.

Try to get a good variety of kindnesses. Examples will be:
- *listening to each other;*
- *smiling at each other;*
- *helping with tasks;*
- *being kind to someone who is upset;*

–   *taking someone for first aid if they have been hurt;*
–   *noticing good things others have done and saying 'That's good.'*

Keep to things that have happened in school. If you allow one child to say 'I invited . . . to my house' or 'to my party', you will get dozens saying the same.

After you have amassed a selection of kindnesses, move on to the next part.

Now, let's think about how kindness works.

Do you do something for someone just because they have done something for you? *(Take answers.)*

That's right. Sometimes we return a kindness and sometimes we are just kind because we see a kindness needs doing.

Are you only kind to your friends? *(Take answers.)*

That's right. We can be kind to other people too. Sometimes that is how we make a friend.

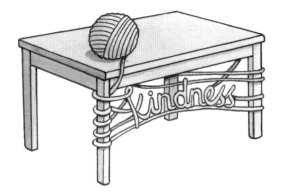

We are kind to people and they are kind to others and those people might be kind to us and so it goes on. Kindness connects us all together.

Let's have a look.

There are two ways of doing this:

(a)   *You can take the safe option, which is to ask a whole class to stand up in a circle and get them to make the web of kindness. It's safe because they will be close and therefore will be very involved with each other.*
(b)   *You can risk making the kindness web with a random group of twenty children from across the school years. Again, stand them in a circle.*

However you choose the children, you need to make a web. Throw the ball of wool to the first child. Ask them to hold the end with one hand. Now they throw the ball to someone who has been kind to them, saying what they did as they throw. It must be someone who is standing up. The person they throw the ball to keeps hold of the thread of wool with one hand, and throws the ball to someone else, detailing the kindness as they throw.

To make this successful you must ensure three things:

(a)   *They throw fast.*

(b)   *They occasionally throw back to people who have already received the wool –
      that makes a better web.*

(c)   *They don't let go of the thread.*

When everyone has got a hold on the wool and there is a good web, stop.

Do you see how we are all connected to each other by kindness? We are all
caught in a web of kindness. That's nice because it means we are not really
ever lonely.

If we stood the whole school in a circle and took all morning to play this game,
we would find that no one was left out.

If we took a year to play this game (and had a very big ball of wool and space
for a very big circle) we would probably find that the whole world was all
connected to each other – through kindness. This is something we need to
remember.

If we ever feel alone, left out or not part of the group, we should remember the
web of kindness we are all caught in. No one is really ever out on their own.

Even if we wanted to, we can't escape the love and kindness in this school.

Bible verses

2 Corinthians 1, v3–4 (Good News Bible).

Let us give thanks to the God and Father of our Lord Jesus Christ, the
merciful Father, the God from whom all help comes! He helps us in all our
troubles, so that we are able to help others who have all kinds of troubles,
using the same help that we ourselves have received from God.

Prayer

Dear Lord, you know we all belong to each other and you know we all
belong to you. Please remind us of this if ever we feel lonely. Please nudge
us if you see a chance for us to be kind. Help us to keep on making the
web. Amen

Thought for the day

Let us try especially hard to notice all the kindnesses done to us. Let us
also try to notice opportunities for us to be kind. Let us make the web
really dense so no one is ever left alone outside it.

This little light of mine

Theme

Smiling at each other does not diminish us but increases the sum total of kindness in our school.

Preparation

You need one long dinner candle, one candlestick and at least twenty cheap household candles, plus a box of matches. It's not a good idea to use a big church or pillar candle as it will be awkward to manoeuvre when you come to use it to light another candle.

The assembly

This assembly is quite short but visually memorable.

Close any curtains or blinds you may have. Make the hall or wherever you are holding the assembly as dark as possible.

Light the large dinner candle, put it in a candlestick and place it in a prominent position at the front. Guard it with your life.

Play quiet music as the children file into the hall. Stand behind the lighted candle, smile and look really cheerful.

Good morning, it's very dark in here, isn't it? I hope you can see me.

I also hope you can see me smiling. Why am I smiling? Well, because smiling is better than scowling and looking a right misery, isn't it?

Sometimes we forget to smile. I know it's hard to smile when there is something really wrong or we are really sad, but sometimes we forget to smile even when there is nothing badly wrong.

Smiling is catching! If someone smiles at you it makes you feel happier; it makes you feel liked. So smiling is something we should try to do as often as possible.

There is a poem I know about this. It goes like this. *(You will need to hold the candle up so you can read this. Don't be tempted to turn the lights on.)*

A smile is like a candle flame,
 Its light gives out a glow
That makes the world seem warmer
And helps a friendship grow.
It lifts away the misery,
The coldness and the dark;
So smile, and see a miracle,
As the flames of friendship spark.

When someone smiles, it lights up their face, and when that smile is caught by someone else, it lights up their face too. Like this.

Now choose twenty sensible children, of different ages, and give them each an unlit candle– a cardboard guard for each candle may be useful. Ask them to sit on the ends of rows on both sides of the hall, going from front to back of the hall. They need to sit on the ends of rows because picking their way around the hall across other children's feet while carrying lit candles would be very dangerous.

Take your lit candle and go up to the child in the front row on the left, and give them a smile. Now light their candle from yours. Then go across to the child in the front row on the right, give them a smile and light their candle from yours.

That's made the hall a bit lighter.

(Speak to the children with the newly lit candles.) Now go to the child behind you, give them a smile and light their candle. Then carefully walk up to the front and stand next to me.

As the smile goes back up the hall and more and more candles are lit and the children walk to the front, you should be in an increasing pool of light.

When you light another candle from yours, it takes nothing away from your candle.

It's like a smile, it costs you nothing, no effort, no pain, just gain!

As the candles are lit you can remark upon the increasing brightness in the room. When all twenty-one of you are standing at the front, look at the school and tell them this.

Those of us who smiled at each other are standing in the light.

It's warm and it's bright. You can see us glow. Let us see if this week we can all try to smile at each other quietly.

You might want to read the poem again at this point.

Let's see if we can lift the darkness and increase the light and the warmth.

Keep the lights off and the candles lit.

Bible verse

John 8, v12 (NIV).
When Jesus spoke again to the people, he said, 'I am the light of the world. Whoever follows me will never walk in darkness, but will have the light of life.'

Prayer

Dear Lord, help us all to be a light in our school. Help us all to make the effort to smile with kindness at those with whom we share our lives. Amen

At the end of this assembly, play quiet music and send the classes out while the children with the candles stand silently at the front, in a pool of light.

So long and thanks for all the fish (Lesson from fishing 2)

Theme

This assembly is like the end-of-term test. It asks children to work out a meaning for it themselves.

Preparation

This assembly can be done by Key Stage 1 or Key Stage 2.

You don't have to do any preparation for this assembly at all. I suggest that you ask the Year 4, 5 and 6 class teachers to be present.

If you want to animate this assembly you can have a couple of children, of any age, to act out the part of the fishermen. To do this you will need two nets, two fishing rods and lots of paper fish, some large and some small. If the paper fish have strings attached to them, some of the younger children could have the job of pulling them along the river.

The assembly

Now, as you know, assemblies usually have two parts. There is the fun part with the action, music, drama and so on, and then there is the serious bit where I explain the real message of the fun bit. The message is there to guide us and help us to live as our best selves.

Well, you have had a lot of help over the years with the messages. I think now it's time that you worked out a message for yourselves.

Today, I am going to tell you a story and you are going to work out a meaning. But what is really amazing is that there is no right answer!

I hope that you can work out two or three different thoughts for the week from the story instead.

Either read this story or arrange for a couple of children to act it out as you read it.

The story is a simple one. Two fishermen sat on the riverbank trying to catch fish.

Fishing is a long, slow business and they were there all day.

Clouds passed by, the sun shone, it rained, the wind blew, birds sang in trees and then flew away.

Fish swam down the stream. Eventually the first fisherman caught a small fish. He pulled it out and looked at it. It was a grey one. He plopped it in his net.

When the second fisherman had a bite he pulled out his fish. It was really big. He looked at it and then threw it back in again.

The next time the fishermen had a bite, the first fisherman caught a big green fish. He pulled it out and plopped it in his net. The second fisherman caught a small red one. He looked at it and threw it back in the river. The same happened every time they caught a fish: one of the fishermen plopped his fish in his net. The other looked at his fish and then threw it back.

More clouds passed by, the sun shone and it rained again. The wind blew, birds sang in the trees and then flew away. More fish swam down the stream.

Then the fishermen went home.

Now, what do you think the story might be about?

If we reflect carefully about the story, can we think of any messages from the fishermen's day by the riverbank? What meaning would you say the story carried?

You will now need to take suggestions and encourage discussion. All suggestions are equally valid, as long as they relate to the story. Younger children will have simple messages, older children more complex ones. Accept them all. Encourage the staff to join in as well.

Remember there is no right answer.

At the end of the assembly there is no prayer and no Bible reading.

Instead, ask the children to find some time during the week to think about some of their suggestions and, in their own time, write prayers and thoughts for the day and find appropriate Bible readings themselves. You could use a centrally placed noticeboard for a display of the story and the assorted meanings generated by the children. This would also be the place for them to put up their related prayers, thoughts and Bible readings.

Children would be able to come along and read each other's ideas. You could then share these ideas, thoughts, prayers and readings during the next week's assembly.

Training from Stay Cool in School

Margaret and Dennis Goldthorpe run an INSET training company called Stay Cool in School.

If you would like further information about training for your school on any of the following topics:
• Circle Time;
• a whole-school approach to encouraging self-discipline;
• dealing with difficult people;
• teaching RE through Circle Time;
• livelier assemblies;

please contact:

Margaret Goldthorpe
Stay Cool in School
Midsummer Cottage
Moor Lane
Sarratt
Hertfordshire
WD3 6BY

01923 262586

dgoldthorpe@onetel.net.uk